WRITERS AND THEIR WORK

ISOBEL ARMSTRONG
General Editor

BRYAN LOUGHREY
Advisory Editor

C.S. LEWIS

C. S. Lewis

photograph by Arthur Strong of C. S. Lewis in his rooms at Magdalen College Oxford, 1947

C. S. LEWIS

William Gray

NORTHCOTE

BRITISH COUNCIL

ATLANTIC
PUBLISHERS & DISTRIBUTORS (P) LTD

Cover picture: by courtesy of HarperCollins/The British Council

This edition is published by

ATLANTIC
PUBLISHERS & DISTRIBUTORS (P) LTD

7/22, Ansari Road, Darya Ganj, New Delhi-110 002
Tel: 40775252, 23273880, 23275880, 23280451; Fax: +91-11-23285873
E-mail: orders@atlanticbooks.com; Web: www.atlanticbooks.com

By arrangement with
Northcote House Publishers Ltd
Horndon House, Horndon, Tavistock, Devon, PL19 9NQ,
United Kingdom. (T)+44(0)1822 810066; (F)+44(0)1822 810034
(E) northcote.house@virgin.net and (W) www.northcotehouse.co.uk
The *Writers and their Work* series is published in association with
the British Council.

First Indian Reprint 2010
First published in 1998 by Northcote House Publishers Ltd

ISBN 978-81-269-1302-2

For sale in the Indian sub-continent only. Not for export elsewhere.

British Library Cataloguing-in-Publication Data
A catalogue record for this book is available from the British Library

Typeset by PDQ Typesetting, Newcastle-under-Lyme
Printed in India at Nice Printing Press, A-33/3A, Site-IV,
Industrial Area, Sahibabad, Ghaziabad, U.P.

Contents

Acknowledgements

I wish to acknowledge the support of my colleagues in the School of English at the Chichester Institute of Higher Education; without them this book would not have happened. Particular thanks go to Margaret, who read some early drafts with a welcome rigour.

This book is dedicated to Joyce, who introduced me to Narnia; to Rebecca, who takes me back there; and to Jonathan, who saved me from my computer (and vice versa).

Biographical Outline

1898 Clive Staples Lewis born to Albert and Florence Lewis in Belfast.

1908 CSL's mother dies in Belfast. Shortly afterwards CSL enrolled at Wynyard School, Watford, England ('Belsen').

1910 Wynyard closed after charges of brutality against the headmaster, who is certified insane the following year.

1914 After attending various schools, CSL is tutored by W. T. Kirkpatrick at Great Bookham, Surrey.

1916 CSL reads George MacDonald's *Phantastes*.

1917 CSL wins scholarship to University College, Oxford. Later this year he joins up, and meets Mrs Janie Moore, the mother of Paddy Moore, with whom he is billeted. In November he is sent to the Front.

1918 CSL wounded in France, and returns to England to convalesce. Paddy Moore killed in action. Mrs Moore visits CSL in various hospitals.

1919 CSL returns to Oxford, and starts living with Mrs Moore and her daughter Maureen. He publishes *Spirits in Bondage*, a collection of poems, under the name of Clive Hamilton.

1922 CSL takes a First in 'Greats' (Classics, Philosophy, and Ancient History), but is unable to find a university teaching post.

1923 CSL takes a First in English Language and Literature, to get 'a second string' to his bow.

1925 CSL elected Fellow of Magdalen College, Oxford.

1926 CSL's long poem *Dymer* published under the name of Clive Hamilton. It is not a success. First recorded meeting with Tolkien.

1929 Death of CSL's father. CSL espouses theism (but not yet orthodox Christianity).

1931 Shortly after a momentous discussion with Tolkien and Hugo Dyson about 'Myth', CSL converts to Christianity.

1933 Publication of *The Pilgrim's Regress.*

1936 Publication of *The Allegory of Love.* CSL meets Charles Williams.

1938 Publication of *Out of the Silent Planet.*

1939 Publication of *Rehabilitations* (a collection of essays including 'Bluspels and Flalansferes') and (with E. M. W. Tillyard) *The Personal Heresy.*

1940 Publication of *The Problem of Pain.* First weekly meeting of 'the Inklings'.

1941 First series of radio talks (later published as *Mere Christianity,* book I).

1942 Further series of radio talks (later published as *Mere Christianity* books II and III). Publication of *The Screwtape Letters* and *A Preface to 'Paradise Lost'.* First meeting of Oxford University Socratic Club.

1943 Publication of *Perelandra* and *The Abolition of Man.*

1944 Further radio talks (later published as *Mere Christianity,* book IV).

1945 Publication of *That Hideous Strength.* Death of Charles Williams.

1946 Publication of *The Great Divorce.*

1947 Publication of *Miracles.*

1948 Debate with Elizabeth Anscombe about chapter III of *Miracles.* CSL seems to many present at the Socratic Club to have lost the argument.

1950 Publication of *The Lion, the Witch and the Wardrobe.* Mrs Moore has to move into a nursing home. Joy Davidman Gresham starts to write to CSL from the USA.

1951 Publication of *Prince Caspian.* Mrs Moore dies.

1952 Publication of *The Voyage of the 'Dawn Treader'.* Joy Gresham visits CSL in Oxford.

1953 Publication of *The Silver Chair.* Joy Gresham moves to England.

1954 CSL accepts Chair of Medieval and Renaissance English at Cambridge University. Publication of *The Horse and His Boy* and *English Literature in the Sixteenth Century.* Joy and

William Gresham are divorced.

1955 Publication of *The Magician's Nephew* and *Surprised by Joy*.

1956 CSL and Joy Gresham are married in the Oxford Registry Office. Six months later Joy is found to have cancer. Publication of *The Last Battle* and *Till We Have Faces*.

1957 CSL and Joy married in a religious ceremony in an Oxford hospital. Joy is believed to be dying.

1958 Joy's cancer is in remission. Publication of *Reflections on the Psalms*.

1959 Joy's cancer returns.

1960 Joy dies. Publication of *The Four Loves*.

1961 Publication of *A Grief Observed* (under the name of N. W. Clerk) and *An Experiment in Criticism*. CSL becomes ill.

1962–3 CSL in poor health but continues to write, producing *Letters to Malcolm* and *The Discarded Image*, both of which are published posthumously in 1964.

1963 Death of CSL.

Abbreviations

AGO	*A Grief Observed* (London: Faber, 1966)
AMR	*All My Road Before Me* (London: Collins Fount, 1993)
AOL	*The Allegory of Love* (London: Oxford University Press, 1938)
AOM	*The Abolition of Man* (London: Collins Fount, 1978)
CR	*Christian Reflections* (London: Collins Fount, 1981)
CT	*The Cosmic Trilogy* (London: Pan Books, The Bodley Head, 1989)
D.	*Dymer* (London: Dent, 1926)
DI	*The Discarded Image* (Cambridge: Cambridge University Press, 1964)
EIC	*An Experiment in Criticism* (Cambridge: Cambridge University Press, 1961)
EL	*English Literature in the Sixteenth Century Excluding Drama* (Oxford: Clarendon Press, 1954)
FL	*The Four Loves* (London: Geoffrey Bles, 1960)
GD	*The Great Divorce* (London: Collins Fontana, 1972)
GMA	*George MacDonald: An Anthology* (London: Geoffrey Bles, 1946)
HHB	*The Horse and His Boy* (London: HarperCollins Diamond, 1997)
L.	*Letters of C. S. Lewis*, ed. W. Hooper (London: Collins Fount, 1988)
LB	*The Last Battle* (London: HarperCollins Diamond, 1997)
LTM	*Letters to Malcolm: Chiefly on Prayer* (London: Collins Fount, 1977)
LWW	*The Lion, the Witch and the Wardrobe* (London: HarperCollins Diamond, 1997)

M.	*Miracles: A Preliminary Study* (London: Geoffrey Bles, 1947)
M.[2]	*Miracles* (London: Collins Fontana, 1960)
MC	*Mere Christianity* (London: Collins Fontana, 1955)
MN	*The Magician's Nephew* (London: HarperCollins Diamond, 1997)
OTOW	*Of This and Other Worlds* (London: Collins, 1982)
PC	*Prince Caspian* (London: HarperCollins Diamond, 1997)
PH	*The Personal Heresy* (London: Oxford University Press, 1939)
PP	*The Problem of Pain* (London: Collins Fontana, 1957)
PPL	*A Preface to Paradise Lost* (London: Oxford Paperbacks, 1960)
PR	*The Pilgrim's Regress* (London: Collins Fount, 1977)
SBJ	*Surprised by Joy* (London: Collins Fontana, 1959)
SC	*The Silver Chair* (London: HarperCollins Diamond, 1997)
SL	*The Screwtape Letters* (London: Collins Fontana, 1955)
SLE	*Selected Literary Essays* (Cambridge: Cambridge University Press, 1969)
SMRL	*Studies in Medieval and Renaissance Literature* (Cambridge: Cambridge University Press, 1966)
TAP	*They Asked for a Paper* (London: Geoffrey Bles, 1962)
TST	*They Stand Together* (London: Collins, 1979)
TWHF	*Till We Have Faces* (London: Collins Fount, 1978)
U.	*Undeceptions* (London: Geoffrey Bles, 1971)
VDT	*The Voyage of the 'Dawn Treader'* (London: HarperCollins Diamond, 1997)

Introduction

C. S. Lewis might well have considered the present book heretical. This is not because it is theologically suspect, but because, in one of his earlier books, *The Personal Heresy,* written with E. M. W. Tillyard, Lewis attacked the assumption that poetry (and by implication other kinds of imaginative writing) is primarily an expression of the inner life of the writer. In a move which anticipated by some years the famous essay by Wimsatt and Beardsley, 'The Intentional Fallacy' (1946), and even in some respects Roland Barthes's 'The Death of the Author' (1968), Lewis denied that the reading of literature is in the first place a matter of '*knowing* or *getting into touch with*', a writer (*PH* 9, emphasis in original). Rather, he maintained, 'when we read poetry as poetry should be read, we have before us no representation which claims to be the poet, and frequently no representation of a *man*, a *character*, or a *personality* at all' (*PH* 4, emphasis in original). Echoing T. S. Eliot's theory of 'impersonality' in literature (though Lewis had to be reminded by Tillyard of his unacknowledged closeness to Eliot on this point, cf. *PH* 31–2), Lewis saw 'poetless poetry' not as an accident of history but rather as an ideal to be aspired to (*PH* 18 ff.). Acutely aware of the split between the self that produces a text and the self that appears *in* the text, Lewis prescribed the suppression of the former as a matter of spiritual hygiene: 'The character whom I describe as myself leaves out... this present act of description – which is an element in my real history; and that is the beginning of a rift which will grow wider at every step we take from the vulgarity of confession to the disinfected and severer world of lyric poetry' (*PH* 10).

This need on Lewis's part to efface the writer in 'real history' has, as we shall see, deep psychological as well as theological roots. It contrasts sharply with the proliferation of Lewis hagiography – the 'Lewis industry' which Kathryn Lindskoog savages in her book *The C. S. Lewis Hoax*. Neither approach – author elimination or author worship – augurs well for a book in the 'Writers and their Work' series. Nevertheless there are suggestions in Lewis's writings of ways in which an awareness of the writer can enhance the appreciation of the work. Although he declared: 'The poet is not a man who asks me to look at *him*' (*PH* 11), there was a famous occasion (his inaugural lecture at Cambridge) when he did call upon the audience precisely to look at him, not admittedly as a poet, nor even necessarily as critic, but as a specimen of what he called with deliberate provocation 'Old Western man' ('De Descriptione Temporum', *SLE*, 13–14). Lewis's resistence to focusing attention on the author rather than on the text by no means precluded taking into account the author's historical context – indeed his best critical work succeeds brilliantly in exposing the reader to the sheer otherness of medieval culture. In the case of Lewis himself, it is important to put his writing in context; to see him not perhaps as a specimen of 'Old Western man', but rather as one of those who perceived more acutely than most the implications of the new movements in philosophy and literary theory in the 1930s and 1940s. An important part of what C. S. Lewis perceived he called 'the Abolition of Man'. The so-called anti-humanisms of poststructuralism and postmodernism would not have surprised him; he saw them coming. In their place he offers a deeply humanistic vision, doubtless a flawed humanistic vision, still perhaps needing to be purged in the acids of postmodernity, but also more aware than one might expect of the groundless abyss of 'the bad infinite'. Indeed Lewis's deeply Platonic 'longing for a Form', a form achieved in *narrative*, is arguably relevant today precisely because he knew the 'horror' and 'torment' of 'the bad infinite' (cf. 'William Morris', *SLE* 228). And if, as he says of Morris in the 1930s, Lewis is currently 'among the labelled' (i.e. out of fashion) in many literary circles, despite or perhaps because of his popularity elsewhere, it may be time to consider the rehabilitation of a writer whose life and work were constituted, as he insisted, by 'a dialectic of desire', and for whom 'the problem of subjectivity' was central. That the dialectic and the problem were lived through, if not perhaps finally resolved, in Christian faith, by no means diminishes the relevance of this writer and his work to current debates about the place of humanist values in a postmodern context.

1

The Quest for Joy (or the Dialectic of Desire)

Despite Lewis's disdain for 'the vulgarity of confession' with its roots in the 'real history' of the author, there is in fact a strong confessional dimension to much of his writing. This is true not only of *Surprised by Joy: The Shape of my Early Life*, but also of his first published prose work, the autobiographical allegory *The Pilgrim's Regress*. In the important Preface which Lewis added to the third edition of the latter book, ten years after its first publication, he tried to remedy its 'needless obscurity', and added that:

> The sole merit I claim for this book is that it written by one who has proved them [various illusions about the real object of Desire] all to be wrong. There is no room for vanity in the claim: I know them to be wrong not by intelligence but by experience, such experience as would not have come my way if my youth had been wiser, more virtuous, and less self-centred than it was. (*PR* 13)

Here Lewis is going outside the text, and pointing to himself, with a vengeance. Such 'vulgarity' might be excused because the Preface *is* literally outside the text, and has a strongly practical and didactic purpose. As Lewis says: 'In this preface the autobiographical element in John [the hero] has had to be stressed because the source of the obscurities lay there. But you must not assume that everything in the book is autobiographical. I was attempting to generalise, not to tell people about my own life' (*PR* 21).

Despite his disclaimer in the short Preface to *Surprised by Joy*, Lewis's autobiographical writing, both there and in *The Pilgrim's Regress*, is similar to the *Confessions* of Augustine (if not those of the 'vulgar' Rousseau) in that it has an explicit theological motivation. In the case of both Lewis and Augustine the writer *is* pointing to himself, but only the better to show the object of his vision and desire – that is, he believes, God. The opposition in *The Personal Heresy* between looking at the poet and looking with the poet's eyes seems here to break down, since we are being invited to look at the poet in order ultimately to see the vision of God. For God's sake look at me, the writer is in effect saying. This subsumption of the writer's self in 'real history' by the self constructed in the 'grand narrative' of God has a theological necessity, whatever other motivations may be at work. To adapt an aside by Sartre on Victor Hugo, it seems that Lewis may really have believed that he was 'C. S. Lewis'. But the self in 'real history' which has been repressed has a tendency to return to problematize the self written up in the 'grand narrative'. Something of this can be seen in Owen Barfield's gentle question in the Introduction to *Light on C. S. Lewis* as to whether there was not in Lewis – without any 'taint of insincerity' – something *voulu*, a touch of pastiche?[1] We shall see later the extent to which Lewis's life and work were a tissue of allusions. For the moment let us turn to 'the dialectic of Desire' – the *lived* dialectic (*PR* 15) – narrated by Lewis.

Although the experience of, and the quest for, what Lewis called 'Joy' appears in much of his fiction and poetry, there are three main texts where he explicitly articulates what we might call his metaphysics of desire. These are 'The Weight of Glory' (a sermon preached in 1941, and published with other addresses in 1949); the Preface to the third edition of *The Pilgrim's Regress* (1943); and, most fully, *Surprised by Joy* (1955). In the first chapter of the latter Lewis explains what he means by 'Joy':

> It is... an unsatisfied desire which is itself more desirable than any other satisfaction. I call it Joy, which is here a technical term and must be sharply distinguished both from Happiness and from Pleasure. Joy (in my sense) has indeed one characteristic, and one only, in common with them; the fact that anyone who has experienced it will want it again. Apart from that... it might almost equally well be called a particular kind of unhappiness or grief.... I doubt whether anyone who has tasted it would ever, if both were in his power, exchange it for all the pleasures in the world. But then Joy is never in our power and pleasure often is. (*SBJ* 20)

The trigger for an experience of Joy can be in itself quite trivial. For the young 'Jack' Lewis (the name which Lewis gave himself as a small boy, and which stuck for the rest of his life), what prompted his first experiences of Joy were: a flowering currant bush and the memory of a toy garden his brother had made in a biscuit-tin lid; Beatrix Potter's *Squirrel Nutkin*; and some lines by Longfellow:

> I heard a voice that cried
> Balder the beautiful
> Is dead, is dead –
>
> (*SBJ* 19–20)

But the experience when it came was overwhelming. Lewis writes: 'It is difficult to find words strong enough for the sensation which came over me; Milton's 'enormous bliss' of Eden . . . comes somewhere near it'(*SBJ* 19). In the corresponding section of *The Pilgrim's Regress* where the hero John first 'awakes to Sweet Desire' we read simply: 'All the furniture of his mind was taken away' (*PR* 33).

Such experiences might be compared with Joyce's 'epiphanies' or Wordsworth's 'spots of time'. T. S. Eliot's handling of mystical experience in *Four Quartets* also seems a relevant comparison, despite the fact that Eliot and Lewis did not find each other congenial. It is tempting, too, to relate Lewis's accounts of desire to more recent French writing on desire – for example, by Lacan and Kristeva – while their and Barthes's use of the term *jouissance* (often translated 'bliss') seems to fit with Lewis's descriptions of the ecstatic loss of self in Joy. But the connection we can be sure of is the link which runs back through the Romantics (who knew their Plotinus), and Augustine (who also knew his Plotinus), to Plato himself and his doctrine of *eros* or desire. We hear this Platonic tradition speaking when Lewis says in 'The Weight of Glory':

> In speaking of this desire for our own far-off country . . . I feel a certain shyness. I am almost committing an indecency. I am trying to rip open the inconsolable secret in each one of you . . . the secret we cannot hide and cannot tell, though we desire to do both. We cannot tell it because it is a desire for something that has never actually happened in our experience. We cannot hide it because our experience is constantly suggesting it, and we betray ourselves like

> lovers at the mention of a name. Our commonest expedient is to call it beauty and behave as if that settled the matter. (*TAP* 200)

After criticizing Wordsworth's attempts to capture the experience by identifying it with certain moments in his own past – a cheat, says Lewis – he continues:

> What he [Wordsworth] remembered would turn out to be a remembering. The books or the music in which we thought the beauty was located will betray us if we trust to them; it was not *in* them, it only came *through* them, and what came through them was longing. These things – the beauty, the memory of our own past – are good images of what we really desire; but if they are mistaken for the thing itself they turn into dumb idols, breaking the hearts of their worshippers. For they are not the thing itself; they are only the scent of flower we have not found, the echo of a tune we have not heard, news from a country we have never yet visited. (*TAP* 200)

This intense feeling of homesickness and longing Lewis identifies with Romantic *Sehnsucht* or yearning. Such desire for a lost homeland, prompted by the experience of beauty, goes back to Plato's Dialogues, particularly *The Symposium* and *Phaedrus*. What is distinctively Platonic in the above passage is the way Lewis emphasizes that the same things can be either 'good images' or 'dumb idols' depending on the way we respond to them. This corresponds with his view that experiences of Joy, which ultimately point beyond themselves to God, can, if misused and taken as ends in themselves, degenerate into mere 'thrills' (cf. *SBJ* 136). Equally Platonic (and, perhaps, Lacanian) is the emphasis that desire is always questing, longing, lacking; or, as Plato puts it in *The Symposium, eros* is the child of Want. Desire, says Lewis, 'cuts across our ordinary distinctions between wanting and having. To have it is, by definition, a want: to want it, we find, is to have it' (*PR*, 12–13). Lewis repeats this idea in a passage in *Surprised by Joy* which suggests that Joy also makes nonsense of our ordinary distinctions between past, present, and future. To remember 'a longing... which had flowed over from the mind and seemed to involve the whole body' was in effect to possess the desire, but 'only possession in so far as that kind of desire is itself desirable' (*SBJ* 135). Elsewhere in the same book he says simply – again echoing Plato – 'All Joy reminds' (*SBJ* 66).

What Joy reminds us of, the obscure object of our desire, is for

Lewis of course God. He would doubtless have given short shrift to the kind of post-Freudian, poststructuralist reading of desire such as the one offered by Catherine Belsey:

> Desire is in excess of the organism ... In consequence it has no settled place to be. And moreover, at the level of the unconscious its objects are no more than a succession of substitutes for an imagined originary presence, a half-remembered 'oceanic' pleasure in the lost real, a completeness which is desire's final unattainable object.[2]

Lewis might have agreed about the succession of substitutes for an imagined originary presence (though not 'imagined' in the sense of 'false'); and also about the half-remembered pleasure in the lost real. What he would have disagreed with is the assumption that desire's final object is unattainable. Lewis became a convert to the Christian faith in the hope that it offered a way home. The succession of substitutes is not necessarily endless ('the bad infinite'); there is a *telos* or End to this wandering, according to Lewis, who thus adopts the heresy (from a postmodern point of view) of Teleology.

Surprised by Joy is a story, a history, of Joy (*SBJ* 134). Yet it is not the story of *a* life, but rather of the two lives which Lewis says he led. These two lives – the 'outer' life in which Lewis included even his 'erotic and ambitious fantasies' (*SBJ* 67), and the 'inner' life exclusively concerned with Joy – had nothing to do with each other, Lewis claims (*SBJ* 97). They are 'oil and vinegar', 'Jekyll and Hyde' (*SBJ* 97) and they 'do not seem to influence each other at all' (*SBJ* 66). If Lewis's 'outer' life, his life in 'real history', is not actually suppressed, it is nevertheless not permitted to contaminate the narrative of his 'inner' life of Joy. The latter is described at one point as 'but momentary flashes, seconds of gold scattered in months of dross, each instantly swallowed up in the old, familiar, sordid, hopeless weariness' (*SBJ* 97–8). When he remembers his 'inner' life, the rest of his life seems merely 'a coarse curtain' (*SBJ* 98). Lewis says that his life was 'perplexed' by this duality (*SBJ* 98). So too, to some extent, is the reader. It seems strange that a writer who lays so much stress on the importance of lived experience should be willing to consign much of that experience to the status of 'dross'. Lewis's 'inner' life was constructed round, and by, literature; he may claim to be presenting the fruits of a 'lived dialectic' of experience, but that experience is always already structured by *literary* or artistic experience. Even his first experience of Joy is prompted by his brother's *toy* garden – a primitive kind of *mimesis* or artistic representation. What is perplexing in all of this is that the experiences in 'real history' which one might suspect are crucially important to 'a history of desire' – for example, his relationship to his mother and the impact on him of her death; his relationship to his father; and whatever sexual relationships he may have had – are all more or less glossed over. It is not that they are not mentioned, but rather that they are not allowed to be significant. Although Lewis argued (not very convincingly) against a rather caricatured version of psychoanalysis (see *PR* 74–86; and the essay, 'Psycho-analysis and Literary Criticism' in *TAP* and *SLE*), some kind of repression does seem to be at work in this apparent need to split his experience into (literary) flashes of gold and (lived) dross. Indeed one of his more perceptive friends threatened to supplement *Surprised by Joy* with a book entitled *Suppressed by Jack* (*TST* 540)!

Much of the material in the Biographical Outline in the present book would probably be consigned to the 'dross' category. It relates merely to the Lewis of 'real history', not to Lewis the raider of the lost Joy. Since Lewis's tale of Joy is very much, as has been suggested, a literary tale, it will be explored further in the next chapter, which is a history of Lewis's reading. In the meantime, it might be worth sifting through the dross of Lewis's life in 'real history' to see whether, despite his determination to deny it any decisive influence on the life that really mattered to him, nevertheless we might find some experiences which perhaps affected him more profoundly than he was willing to acknowledge.

In the first place, one of the things most obviously underplayed in Lewis's autobiography is his Irishness. Born in Ireland, for most of his life Lewis was resident in England, another country which was also not another country, since until the 1920s all of Ireland, and thereafter Northern Ireland, was part of the United Kingdom. Despite his initially hostile reaction to England when he says he 'conceived a hatred for England which it took many years to heal' (*SBJ* 26), there is little evidence in his autobiography of any continuing hatred for England or of any deep sense of exile. It is noticeable that the autobiography of an Irishman, covering the years 1898–1931, should make no mention of the Easter Rising of 1916 and the creation of an independent Irish state. Perhaps the nearest Lewis comes to commenting on 'the Irish question' (and it is still, characteristically, very distanced) is to state in *The Allegory of Love* that he will not attempt to excuse Spenser's involvement in 'a detestable policy in Ireland', the wickedness of which begins to corrupt Spenser's imagination in the fifth book of *The Faerie Queene* (*AOL* 349). One unconscious response to being caught in the real-life double-bind of being Irish, while also wishing to remain British, might have been a certain confusion of identity and a need to escape to less problematic countries of the imagination.

Certainly the resort to imaginary other worlds had been the response of the young Lewis to the intractable problems of his home life. With his brother Warnie he created an imaginary other country in an attic room of 'Little Lea', the rambling house in a Belfast suburb to which the Lewises moved when Lewis was 6 years old. Even before the death of his mother when Lewis was 9 years old – a loss which, as many have noted, was to haunt his life and work – his father was (according to Lewis) a difficult and emotional man. So badly did he take his wife's death that 'under the pressure of anxiety his temper became incalculable; he spoke wildly and acted unjustly. Thus by a peculiar cruelty of fate, during those months the unfortunate man, had he but known it, was really losing his sons as well as his wife' (*SBJ* 21). It is interesting that Lewis describes the alienation between himself and his father only as a loss to his father. His own loss of a father is unacknowledged. The traumatic impact on Jack Lewis of his mother's death is also muted by the rather impersonal manner of its narration. The loss is always spoken of as a loss to 'our family' or to 'us boys'. There is only one point at which Lewis makes reference to his personal experience of loss: 'There came a night when I was ill and crying both with headache and toothache and distressed because my mother did not come to me' (*SBJ* 20). Such a feeling of abandonment by the mother has often been believed by psychoanalysts to do great psychological damage. One does not have to go to the rather extreme lengths of David Holbrook's psychoanalytical readings of Lewis's writings to see reflections of the young Lewis's bereavement in his life and work, and especially in his fantasy writing. The dying mother is explicitly present in *The Magician's Nephew*, and, as we will see below, the White Witch can be read as a dead and dangerous 'Bad Mother', freezing the world and turning people to stone.

The (re)turn to the imaginary when external reality has become unbearable is perhaps the only way of maintaining sanity in certain circumstances. The world of fantasy or Faerie can, as Lewis's close friend J. R. R. Tolkien wrote in 'On Fairy-Stories', bring 'recovery, escape and consolation'. Lewis discovered this as a child, and was to repeat the strategy in later life. How the sense of loss and the turn to the imaginary are related to the experience of Joy is not entirely clear. Lewis explicitly says that he is unsure whether his first experiences of Joy came before or after his mother's death (*SBJ* 20). Certainly both must have occurred around the same time, and it seems unlikely that they are unconnected. 'The Imaginary' is also a technical term used by critics influenced by French psychoanalytic theory following Lacan. It refers to an early stage of psychological development, prior to the fixing of identity that occurs when the infant is inserted into the patriarchal mould formed by language and culture (the so-called Symbolic Order). The earlier stage of 'the Imaginary' is defined by Kristeva in terms of 'what the Self imagines in order to sustain and expand itself'.[3] It is quite close to Catherine Belsey's idea (quoted above) of an 'imagined originary presence...a completeness which is desire's final unattainable object'.[4] That Lewis should have had a feeling of 'enormous bliss', an excess of desire (*SBJ* 19), which was withdrawn at the very moment of its appearing, a feeling which seems partly to be *constituted* by the sense of loss, is difficult to keep apart from our knowledge of his mother's death, which he describes as being like the sinking of the great continent of Atlantis (*SBJ* 23).

The lost mother continued to haunt Lewis's life. After the sinking of another continent, Europe, into the nightmare of the First World War, Lewis turned to a fantasy mother, Mrs Janie Moore. Mrs Moore was the mother of a comrade, Paddy Moore, who died in action. According to Mrs Moore and her daughter Maureen, Lewis and Moore had made a pact to look after the other's surviving parent should either of them be killed (Kathryn Lindskoog has questioned the nature, and even the existence, of such a pact.[5]) The precise nature of Lewis's relation to Janie Moore, with whom he lived for around thirty years, is a matter of much speculation and debate. Owen Barfield, who was perhaps Lewis's closest friend during the relevant period, is quoted by George Sayer as saying that the likelihood that Lewis and Mrs Moore were lovers was 'fifty–fifty'.[6] In a new introduction to the 1997 edition of his book Sayer says that now, after further conversations with Mrs Moore's daughter, he is now 'quite certain' that they were lovers.[7] In A. N. Wilson's view it would be amazing if Lewis's relationship with Mrs Moore had been entirely asexual.[8] There can be no doubt, he says, that Lewis and Mrs Moore fell in love at the end of the First World War when Lewis was convalescing from his wounds and Mrs Moore was frantically awaiting news of her son Paddy, who in the event had been killed.[9] Lindskoog takes a similar line,[10] and even Walter Hooper in his introduction to Lewis's diary, *All My Road Before Me*, admits that 'the notion of sexual intimacy... must be regarded as likely' (*AMR* 9). This consensus seems to be borne out by the following rather ostentatiously evasive passage in *Surprised by Joy*:

> I must warn the reader that one huge and complex episode will be omitted. I have no choice about this reticence. All I can or need say is that my earlier hostility to the emotions was very fully and variously avenged. But even if I were free to tell the story, I doubt if it has much to do with the subject of the book. (*SBJ*, 160)

It is noticeable that once again Lewis denies that even an experience presumably so personal and intense has much bearing on the subject of his book, that is, the story of Joy. And yet, according to *Surprised by Joy*, Joy did vanish, or was excluded, from his life for a period of about twelve years. It returned sometime in 1929, when, as Lewis puts it, 'the long inhibition was over, the dry desert lay behind, I was off once more to the land of longing, my heart at once broken and exalted as it had never been since the old days at Bookham' (*SBJ* 173–4). Characteristically it was the reading of a piece of literature, the *Hippolytus* of Euripides, that precipitated the return of Joy. In the 'joyless' period between the two-and-a-half years he had spent at Great Bookham, Surrey, being tutored by W. T. Kirkpatrick, and the decisive reading of the *Hippolytus*, Lewis had spent first a few months in Oxford, then six months in action in France, where he was wounded; the remainder of the time he was in Oxford, first of all as an undergraduate at University College, and subsequently as a Fellow of Magdalen College. Lewis first met Mrs Moore on his initial brief spell in Oxford, and she visited him regularly after he was invalided home (his father would not budge from Ireland). From the time of his return to Oxford they lived together, a highly dangerous arrangement from the point of view of Lewis's career. Mrs Moore, an Irishwoman, was twenty-seven years older than Lewis, and, at the time he read the *Hippolytus* and Joy flooded back, Lewis must have been around 30 and Mrs Moore around 57 years old. The plot of the *Hippolytus* centres around the eponymous hero's rejection of his stepmother's sexual advances, and his subsequent destruction brought about by his enraged but misinformed father. In whatever way this combination of forbidden love between stepmother and son, a puritanical rejection of erotic love, and murderous patriarchal jealousy were connected with the deeper levels of Lewis's own experiences in 'real history', it is difficult not to feel that somehow they were connected. A further hint at such a connection is the strangely unnecessary appendix to *An Experiment in Criticism* entitled 'A Note on Oedipus', where Lewis talks about 'those not uncommon myths which give the earth-goddess a young consort who is also her son' (*EIC* 142). The appendix seems almost obsessively to repeat variations on the phrase 'a man who married his mother'.

It may be that Lewis's life in 'real history' during this period is mere 'dross', and has, as he says, not much to do with the history of Joy. On the other hand, the absence of Joy is as much part of the story of Joy as its presence. At Bookham Lewis had been an adolescent; by 1929 his relation with his mother–wife was entering a phase when he was still a relatively young man and she was almost an old woman. Lewis always maintained that Joy had nothing to do with sex. It is curious, however, that the absence of Joy seems to coincide with the presence (in all likelihood) of some kind of sexual relationship with Janie Moore. But in the end perhaps we simply have to take Lewis's word for it that the subject of *Surprised by Joy*, his 'inner life' and the quest for Joy, has nothing to do with Lewis in 'real history' or with his 'outer life', including, on his own admission, all his erotic fantasies (*SBJ* 67).

The resurgence of Joy in 1929 is also, according to Lewis's narrative, the beginning of the end of Joy, because the return of Joy marks the start of his conversion, first to theism, and subsequently in 1931 to Christian faith. Just as for St Paul, Christ is the end (*telos*) of the Jewish Law (Rom. 10: 4) in that he both abolishes it and fulfils it, so Christ is for Lewis the end of Joy. Christ is, for the Christian, the decisive appearance (as 'a fact', as Lewis would have said) of that for which (or he for whom) there had previously been only an unconscious longing. In a move which goes back to the early Christian Apologists, Lewis suggests that *eros* and philosophy were to the Greeks what the Law was to the Jews: a tutor or custodian until the coming of Christ. This idea is developed allegorically in *The Pilgrim's Regress*, where the Jewish Law becomes 'the Rules' of 'the Shepherd People' and the 'pagan' desire for the Good becomes the desire for 'pictures'. The 'Sweet Desire' born of these 'pictures' develops into medieval Courtly Love, and later into nineteenth century Romantic nature-worship (*PR* 197 ff.). The longing of the hero John for an Island he has glimpsed is in this tradition of the pagan desire for 'pictures', and is clearly an allegorical presentation of Lewis's own history with Joy. If this pagan 'dialectic of desire' rigorously rejects all those objects of desire which prove in experience to be not what was *really* desired, it *can* (though in only one case in a thousand *does*) reach Christian truth or 'Mother Kirk's chair' (*PR* 196). Similarly, the conclusion of *Surprised by Joy* shows the development of Lewis's delight in myths, and especially myths of dying gods (such as Balder, Adonis, and Bacchus), into a belief that the myth of the dying and rising Christ had 'really happened', that 'here and here only in all time the myth must have become fact' (*SBJ* 189). Crucial to this development was a conversation Lewis had in September 1931 with Tolkien and Hugo Dyson while walking in the grounds of Magdalen College until the early hours of the morning (cf. *TST*, 421, 425, 427–8). This conversation also generated Tolkien's poem 'Mythopoeia', a reply to Lewis's claim that myths or stories were like 'breathing a lie through

Silver'.[11] Nine days later, on a visit to Whipsnade Zoo, Lewis started to believe that Jesus Christ is 'in fact' the Son of God. This rather bizarre setting for his final conversion to Christianity has nevertheless a certain appropriateness. After all, Lewis's main claim to fame, *The Chronicles of Narnia,* centre round the incarnation of the Son of God as a lion in a world of talking animals.

Lewis's story of Joy apparently comes to an end with his conversion. It is not that, like Wordsworth, he no longer feels 'the old stab, the old bitter-sweet' (*SBJ* 190). He does, and as sharply as ever, he says; it is just that Joy 'has lost nearly all interest for me since I became a Christian' (*SBJ* 190). The dialectical structure of Joy – that is, the fact that Joy is always directed towards something other than what immediately prompts it – is itself taken up into a greater dialectic where Joy itself is seen only to have had value 'as a pointer to something other and outer' (*SBJ* 190). With Lewis's conversion in 1931, the quest for Joy seems over, and the dialectic of desire concluded. Yet *Surprised by Joy* does not end on a note of complete closure. Although Lewis is at last on St Augustine's 'high road to that land of peace', and duly grateful to 'the authority' that set up the passing signs (i.e. the stabs of Joy), nevertheless the final sentence of the book is not, as we might have expected, 'We would be at Jerusalem.' The book actually ends with the paragraph: 'Not, of course, that I don't often catch myself stopping to stare at roadside objects of even less importance' (*SBJ* 190).

This could be seen as a kind of deliberate bathos. It could also be seen as symptom of the inherent endlessness of desire, its intrinsic resistance to closure. Like his model St Augustine in the *Confessions,* Lewis presents in *Surprised by Joy* a retrospective narrative of his conversion, from the perspective of orthodoxy, written a good number of years after the events it describes. Both Lewis and Augustine had been brought to Christian faith via the Platonic dialectic of desire. The extent to which that dialectic was truly concluded by conversion is certainly exaggerated in the *Confessions;* Augustine's writings contemporaneous with his conversion are far more Platonic and rather less orthodox than his retrospective narrative suggests. Similarly, it is questionable whether the dialectic of desire was quite as concluded in Lewis's 'real history' as *Surprised by Joy* would have us believe, for the logic of the dialectic of desire goes on forever. And the 'good infinite' of the Platonic endlessness of desire questing ever 'further up and further in' (cf. *LB* 152 ff.) is always liable to transform itself into the 'bad infinite' of the Lacanian endlessness of desire as lack and loss, sliding ever further over and ever further out. If the 'good infinite' of desire can lead, as in the conclusion of *The Last Battle*, to ever more 'real' Narnias, then the 'bad infinite' can lead deeper and deeper into depression and melancholia. Lewis's increasingly aggressive defences of 'the Christian faith' during the 1940s are perhaps defences as much against threatening forces within as against any external enemy. It is arguable, *pace* the conclusion of *Surprised by Joy*, that the dialectic of desire was by no means ended by Lewis's conversion in 1931. Indeed, as we shall see, when *Surprised by Joy* itself was published in 1955, Lewis in 'real history' was perhaps more than ever in quest of Joy.

2

Intertextual Healing

Even as a teenager Jack Lewis was conscious of his tendency to let his reading shape, if not actually replace, his experience of 'real life'. In an early letter to his friend Arthur Greeves he wrote:

> You ask whether I have ever been in love: fool as I am, I am not quite such a fool as that. But if one is only to talk from first hand experience on any subject, conversation would be a very poor business. But though I have no personal experience of the thing they call love, I have what is better – the experience of Sappho, of Euripides, of Catullus, of Shakespeare, of Spenser, of Austen, of Brontë, of, of, – anyone else I have read. (*TST* 85)

Later in *The Personal Heresy* he described literature as 'a voyage beyond the limits of [the reader's as well as the writer's] personal point of view, an annihilation of the brute fact of his own particular psychology rather than its assertion' (*PH* 26–7). And in one of his last books, *An Experiment in Criticism*, Lewis spoke eloquently of:

> the impulse ... to go out of the self, to correct its provincialism and heal its loneliness. In love, in virtue, in the pursuit of knowledge, and in the reception of the arts, we are doing this.... [t]his process can be described either as an enlargement or as a temporary annihilation of the self. But that is an old paradox; 'he that loseth his life shall save it'. ... *Literary experience heals the wound without undermining the privilege of individuality*... I transcend myself; and am never more myself than when I do. (*EIC* 138 ff., emphasis added)

While remaining wary of the tendency to make a kind of religion out of aesthetic experience (cf. 'Christianity and Literature' in *Christian Reflections*), Lewis nevertheless clearly does see the act of reading as at least analogous to certain kinds of religious experience. Literary experience and Joy have a similar relation to Christian faith; as long as neither of them is made into an idolatrous substitute for Christian faith, for Lewis they may provide invaluable experiences which can point towards, and even participate in, the truth of Christianity. This links with Tolkien's argument in 'On Fairy-Stories' that the literary artist is not so much a creator as a *sub*-creator; the artist *imitates* the transcendent creativity of God. But it is the analogy between literary experience and Joy that is of particular interest, since, as has already been suggested, Lewis's history of Joy – that is, the story of the 'inner' life that really mattered to him – is practically identical with the history of his reading. Lewis himself was wary of an undue critical attention to a writer's reading. He calls such an approach 'that deadly outlook... which treats a poet as a mere conduit pipe through which "motifs" and "influences" pass by some energy of their own' ('Neoplatonism in the Poetry of Spenser', *SMRL* 149). Nevertheless Lewis also says that 'a full account of Spenser's reading would perhaps illuminate his work more than an account of his friendships' (*EL* 355). This remark could apply to Lewis himself at least as much as it does to Spenser – who was of course a major source for, and influence on, Lewis. Lewis carefully distinguished between 'source' and 'influence' in an essay on 'The Literary Impact of the Authorised Version', where he writes: 'A Source gives us something to write about; an Influence prompts us to write in a certain way' (*SLE* 133). Thus Lewis says: 'my own habit of immoderate quotation showed the Influence of Hazlitt, but not the Influence of the authors I quote' (*SLE* 134). Spenser therefore is not only a *source* for Lewis, as will become apparent later; he is also an *influence* in that it would be as true to say of Lewis as of Spenser that in his mind 'the fruits of his reading met and mingled and transformed one another' (*EL* 355).

Whether or not it is always possible to distinguish between 'influence' and 'source' as sharply as Lewis wished, it is important nevertheless to attempt some kind of overview of the key 'influences' (if only in a loose sense) on Lewis. Lewis was a voracious and omnivorous reader. While he had his own list of favourite texts which he reread many times, he was in principle against any exclusive literary canon, especially of the kind imposed by what he called in *An Experiment in Criticism* 'the Vigilant school' – a transparent and not uncourageous attack on the followers of F. R. Leavis and his 'Great Tradition' who dominated Cambridge when Lewis taught there. Indeed Lewis championed so-called popular fiction before it became fashionable to do so. But the books which changed, shaped, and indeed in a sense *were* his life are mostly referred to in *Surprised by Joy*. For the purposes of this brief survey I have divided them into four broad categories.

'NORTHERN'

As mentioned above, one of Lewis's earliest experiences of Joy was triggered by his reading of Longfellow's poem 'Tegner's Drapa'. This is a version of the Norse myth of the death and funeral of Balder, the paragon of the Norse gods. Balder's death is brought about through the treachery of the jealous Loki, the subject of a juvenile work by Lewis. It was Lewis's first experience of what he called 'Northernness', 'a vision of huge, clear spaces hanging above the Atlantic in the endless twilight of Northern summer, remoteness, severity...' (*SBJ* 62). After a kind of latency period, this experience of 'almost sickening intensity' (*SBJ* 20) returned with Lewis's discovery of Wagner. At first it was simply the words *Siegfried and the Twilight of the Gods*, glimpsed but barely understood, and some illustrations by Arthur Rackham, which provoked an 'unendurable sense of desire and loss' (*SBJ* 62). Although Lewis went on to discover the words and music of Wagner 'properly', it is the very fleetingness and contingency of the triggers for his early experiences of 'Northernness' which are striking. This links with Lewis's claim in *An Experiment in Criticism* that 'myth' has a power and value 'independent of its embodiment in any literary work' (*EIC* 41). The power of myth, whether Norse, Greek, or modern (such as Stevenson's *Dr Jekyll and Mr Hyde* or Kafka's *The Castle*), resists all attempts to grasp it conceptually, for example, by means of allegorical explanation. The experience of myth is, according to Lewis, awe-inspiring and numinous (*EIC* 44). It is this power of myth to 'suggest something important' which cannot be conceptualized (*EIC* 45), that informed Lewis's turn from writing rational defences of Christianity to the writing of *The*

Chronicles of Narnia (it also suggests why Lewis resisted calling the Narnia books allegories). *The Chronicles of Narnia* are the result of the mingling and transformation of various myths. There is, however, a strong element of 'Northernness' in the mix – for example, in the dwarfs and the giants (especially the great Time-giant), and most explicitly in the American edition of *The Lion, the Witch and the Wardrobe*, where the Captain of the Witch's Secret Police is called Fenris Ulf after the Norse Fenris Wolf, and there is explicit reference to the World Ash Tree ('Yggdrasil' in Norse mythology).[1]

GREEK

The piece of Lewis juvenilia mentioned above, his tragedy *Loki Bound*, is a strange hybrid: Norse in subject, but Greek in form. For the young Lewis 'Northernness' still came first, though the Norse myth was now presented in a form whose careful imitation of all the elements of Greek tragedy was 'as classical as any Humanist could have desired' (*SBJ* 94). This juvenile work reflects Lewis's new enthusiasm for classical literature and especially Euripides' *Bacchae*, in the reading of which 'a new quality entered my imagination: something Mediterranean and volcanic, the orgiastic drum-beat' (*SBJ* 93). The *Bacchae* was to have a lasting influence on Lewis, as can be seen in the extended description of a Bacchanalian procession near the end of *Prince Caspian*. The impact on Lewis of Euripides' *Hippolytus* has already been mentioned; again it is the emotional power of Euripides' drama that is foregrounded by Lewis. Whereas Nietzsche in *The Birth of Tragedy* criticized the rationalism of Euripides, Lewis's reading of the *Hippolytus* precipitated the crumbling of his attempt to maintain a cool, rationalistic distance from an emotional response to life. In his own phrase he was 'overwhelmed' by the return of Joy occasioned by the play (*SBJ* 173).

Nor was Lewis's Platonism cool and 'philosophical' in the modern sense; as he realized in the company of Owen Barfield and Alan (later Bede) Griffiths, 'philosophy wasn't a *subject* to Plato' (*SBJ* 180). Apart from the explicitly Platonist ending of *The Last Battle*, where Digory (now Professor) Kirke says: 'It's all in

Plato, all in Plato' (*LB* 160), there is also a crucial dialogue in *Silver Chair* where the heroes (Jill, Eustace, Puddleglum, and the Prince) debate with the Queen of Underland about whether it is the world inside or outside the cave which is real. The Queen argues that the sun in what she calls the imaginary outer world is merely a make-believe copy of a lamp in 'real' Underland (*SC* 141–2). This reworking of the Cave allegory in Plato's *Republic* is addressing the question of how we know, in an ultimate sense, which is the Copy and which is the Original. This question has far-reaching implications, because for Lewis modern materialistic ways of thinking make the (for him) unwarranted assumption that the 'higher' (the 'spiritual') is always a reflection or production or 'copy' of the 'lower' (the 'material'). More specifically, Joy, or spiritual experience generally, is seen as a substitute for, or a sublimation of, something material, that is, sex (or, as Lewis crudely puts it in a letter to his friend Arthur Greeves, Joy is for the psychoanalyst 'a defecated masturbation which fancy gives one to compensate for external chastity' (*TST* 338)). Lewis is never more Platonist than when, in his dialectic of desire, he inverts this assumption: 'Joy is not a substitute for sex; sex is very often a substitute for Joy. I sometimes wonder whether all pleasures are not substitutes for Joy (*SBJ* 138; cf. *TST* 338–9).

'MEDIEVAL'

Malory's *Le Morte D'Arthur* and Spenser's *The Faerie Queene* are often cited as literary works which made a significant impact on Lewis. Clearly both books contributed to the 'medieval' atmosphere which Lewis created in *The Chronicles of Narnia*. *The Faerie Queene* is, of course, technically not a medieval work at all, belonging rather to the period usually called 'The Renaissance', though Lewis refused to use this term in *English Literature in the Sixteenth Century* because 'a word of such wide and fluctuating meaning is of no value' (*EL* 55). Nevill Coghill recalls a chance encounter with Lewis, who suddenly announced to the astonished Coghill: 'I *believe* I have proved that the Renaissance never happened in England. *Alternatively* that if it did, *it had no importance*!' (emphasis in original).[2] On other occasions Lewis was willing to use the term 'Renaissance', if only to show how the opposition between 'Medieval' and 'Renaissance' breaks down in the case of Spenser, who was 'something between the last of the medieval poets and the first of the romantic medievalists, [who produced] a tale...more redolent of the past...than any real medieval romance [and denied] in his own person, the breach between the Middle Ages and the Renaissance' (*SMRL* 148).

In his work as a literary historian and critic Lewis probably devoted more attention to Spenser than to any other writer. The book which in 1936 first made his name was his brilliant *The Allegory of Love: A Study in Medieval Tradition*, which culminates in a lengthy chapter on *The Faerie Queene*. Thirty-one years later Lewis's *Spenser's Images of Life* was published posthumously. Many of the critical and historical works he published between these two books contain substantial discussions of Spenser. In a professional sense Lewis's investment in Spenser was enormous, yet the piece on Spenser that is most revealing for our present purposes is a very short work called 'On Reading *The Faerie Queene*'. It begins: 'Beyond all doubt it is best to have made one's first acquaintance with Spenser in a very large – and, preferably, illustrated – edition of *The Faerie Queene*, on a wet day, between the ages of twelve and sixteen...' (*SMRL* 146). There are, he says, many aspects to *The Faerie Queene*, including a 'luxurious, Italianate and florid' Renaissance element, but:

> it is best to begin with a taste for the homespun...and to keep your *Faerie Queene* on the same shelf with Bunyan and Malory...and even with *Jack the Giant-Killer*...For this is the paradox of Spenser's poem; it is not really medieval – no medieval romance is very like it – yet everyone who has really enjoyed it...has enjoyed it as the very consummation of the Middle Ages...' (*SMRL* 147)

In a previous essay Lewis had argued that what *The Faerie Queene* requires of the reader is not critical acumen but a 'childlike attention to the mood of the story' (*SMRL* 137), because 'its primary appeal is to the most naïve and innocent tastes: to that level of our consciousness which is divided only by the thinnest veil from the immemorial lights and glooms of the collective Unconscious itself. It demands of us a child's love of marvels and dread of bogies, a boy's [*sic*] thirst for adventures' (*SMRL* 132–3).

Apart from its intrinsic interest, it is also worth quoting Lewis on *The Faerie Queene* because his work as a critic leads directly into his work as the writer of *The Chronicles of Narnia*. As A. N. Wilson puts it: 'in showing us what he loves about *The Faerie Queene*... Lewis is actually writing a recipe for how to construct the Narnia Chronicles';[3] another critic refers to the Narnia books simply as Lewis's 'miniature *Faerie Queene*'.[4]

'ROMANTIC'

Lewis had already discovered the writings of William Morris before he read Malory and Spenser. Although Morris is probably best known for his 'romantic medievalism', there is a strong element of 'Northernness' in his writing, and it was Lewis's interest in Norse mythology which had first led him to Morris's translations of Icelandic literature. 'Almost with a sense of disloyalty', Lewis says, he realized that 'the letters WILLIAM MORRIS were coming to have at least as potent a magic in them as WAGNER' (*SBJ* 132; capitals in original). Morris's poetry failed to satisfy Lewis, however, and it was the 'medieval' prose romances, such as *The Well at the World's End*, that were to have a decisive influence on his own writing, especially in *The Chronicles of Narnia*. Indeed the very title *The Well at the World's End* had a powerful impact. As Lewis puts it in his essay 'On Stories':

> it must be understood that this series [of events] – the *plot* as we call it – is only really a net whereby to catch something else. The real theme may be... something that has no sequence in it, something other than a process, and much more like a state or quality. Giantship, otherness, the desolation of space, are examples... The titles of some stories illustrate the point very well. *The Well at the World's End* – can a man write a story to that title? Can he find a series of events... which will really catch and fix and bring home to us all that we grasp at on merely hearing the six words?... I must confess that the net very seldom does suceed in catching the bird. Morris in *The Well at the World's End* came near to sucess – quite near enough to make the book worth many readings. (*OTOW* 42–3)

Once again Lewis might almost be talking about his own science-fiction trilogy, and the Narnia sequence.

To call William Morris's work 'romantic' is obviously to use the term in a broad sense. Lewis consistently problematized literary periodization, as was noted above in relation to 'the Renaissance'. In the Preface to *The Pilgrim's Regress* he discriminated between seven different ways of being 'romantic'. Although many authors, Morris included, are 'romantic' in more than one sense, the kind of 'Romanticism' into which Morris most obviously fits is Lewis's second category (the one which Lewis himself 'always loved') – that is, 'the marvellous', which includes 'magicians, ghosts, fairies, witches, dragons, nymphs, and dwarfs', provided they do not 'make part of a believed religion' (*PR* 10). Lewis's list of authors who are 'romantic' in this sense includes Malory, Boiardo, Ariosto, and Spenser, as well as Morris. Of the other 'romantic' figures who decisively influenced Lewis only Wordsworth belonged to the Romantic period proper.

Two other 'romantic' poets should be mentioned before moving on to Lewis's acknowledged master, George MacDonald. Wordsworth is perhaps a rather strange omission from Lewis's category of romanticism as 'egoism and subjectivism'. 'Egoism' can, of course, be distinguished from 'egotism', but it seems odd to overlook the poet for whom Keats coined the phrase 'the egotistical sublime'. Lewis's attitude to Wordsworth seems ambivalent, perhaps because he was to some extent aware of the similarities between Wordsworth and himself that others have noted. A. N. Wilson talks of the need 'to understand the kind of writer Lewis was – a Romantic egoist [*sic*] in the tradition of Wordsworth and Yeats'.[5] *The Prelude* was one of Lewis's favourite poems, yet in *Surprised by Joy* (whose title is plagiarized from Wordsworth's famous sonnet), and in the sermon 'The Weight of Glory' cited above, he is critical of Wordsworth's 'mistake' or 'cheat' in trying to possess 'Joy' by possessing a moment in the past (*SBJ* 135; *TAP* 200). Wordsworth's premature fixing of the dialectic of desire was perhaps too close to Lewis for comfort. Another poet included in the 'romantic' pantheon of Lewis's adolescence is W. B. Yeats, who 'revivified and transmuted that romantic tradition which he found almost on its death-bed' (Preface to *D.*, p. xiv). But Yeats 'unlike other romantic poets, really and literally believed in the sort of beings he put into his poems' (*D.*, p. xii); he 'stood apart from the rest' because 'he believed seriously in Magic' (*SBJ*, 141). Lewis, who as an undergraduate had twice been admitted to Yeats's house in Oxford, 'was overawed by his personality, and by his doctrine half fascinated and half repelled' (*D.*, p. xiii). What Yeats represented for the young Lewis was the possibility that Joy could be found in the Occult and through the practice of magic. But to Lewis, after some amateurish dabbling, this seemed as much of an illusion as the temptation to reach Joy through sex; the Devil, he says, could no more deliver 'the real Desirable' than could the Flesh (*SBJ* 145–6).

The writer who really did change Lewis's life was George MacDonald (1824–1905). Early in 1916 Lewis picked up from the station bookstall at Bookham a copy of MacDonald's *Phantastes: A Faerie Romance* (1858), without, he says, having the faintest idea what he had let himself in for (*SBJ* 146). He was already 'waist deep in Romanticism', but *Phantastes,* though 'romantic enough in all conscience', was different (Preface to *GMA* 20). In a way which exemplifies the analogy, made earlier in this chapter, between reading and religious experience, Lewis calls his encounter with *Phantastes* 'the baptism of his imagination'. It was as if he had died 'in the old country' and come alive again in a new, in another, country. In one sense everything was familiar; he found all that had charmed him in Malory, Spenser, Morris, and Yeats (*SBJ* 145). Yet there was a new quality, a 'bright shadow', which he would later call 'Holiness' (*SBJ* 145). In an extraordinary and revealing passage Lewis describes his encounter with this 'Holiness' experienced in the act of reading *Phantastes*:

> For the first time the song of the sirens sounded like the voice of my mother or my nurse... It was as if the voice which had called to me from the world's end were now speaking at my side. It was with me in the room, or in my own body, or behind me. If it had once eluded me by its distance, it now eluded me by proximity – something too near to see, too plain to be understood, on this side of knowledge. It seemed to have been always with me; if I could ever have turned my head quick enough I should have seized it. (*SBJ* 145)

This evocation of 'the primary maternal matrix' or what Kristeva calls 'the semiotic *chora*' – that is, the original ungraspable experience of the mother's voice and body which underlies all subsequent experience and identity caught in the net of the so-called Symbolic Order – is all the more remarkable because it is a response to *MacDonald's* writing. What Lewis could not have known when he first read *Phantastes* was that MacDonald had lost his mother at about the same age as Lewis had lost his. MacDonald's writing, and particularly *Phantastes,* is haunted by the loss of his mother, powerfully if not explicitly.[6] Without consciously knowing this, Lewis responded to what he called 'a certain quality of Death' in MacDonald's work (*GMA* 21).

MacDonald's talent as a *writer* was not overestimated by Lewis, but, as a maker of myth or fantasy in the genre of works by Novalis or Kafka, MacDonald ranked for Lewis as 'the greatest genius' (Preface to *GMA* 16). Lewis regarded him as his master; 'indeed,' he says, 'I fancy I have never written a book in which I did not quote from him' (*GMA* 20). In a bold piece of intertextuality that borders on the bizarre, MacDonald appears *in propria persona* in Lewis's *The Great Divorce*, figuring as Virgil to Lewis's Dante. There are many ways in which MacDonald's influence can be seen at work in Lewis's writing; perhaps the most important for Lewis's Narnia books is the movement *between* worlds, which MacDonald had learned from the fantasy literature of German Romanticism (e.g. Novalis, Hoffmann, and Tieck), in which he was as much at home as in the English Romantic tradition.

3

Telling it Slant: The Allegorical Imperative

OUTING THE ALLIGATOR

Even if C. S. Lewis had never written the Narnia books, he would still be celebrated (at least in literary circles) as the author of *The Allegory of Love*. This book has set the agenda for critical discussion of *The Faerie Queene* for sixty years. For example, in her book *Desire*, published in 1994, Catherine Belsey, not the most willing bedfellow of C. S. Lewis, not only orientates her argument by reference to Lewis's reading of *The Faerie Queene*. but finds it 'hard to resist the outlines of the story he tells'.[1] Lewis did not just make an outstanding contribution to a field of literary study; it would hardly be an exaggeration to say that he almost single-handedly *constituted* a field of literary study. 'The Alligator of Love', as Lewis liked to call his famous book, is not only a marvellously informative account of its subject; it is also so compulsively readable that one can well believe the advice reportedly given to an Oxford undergraduate by his tutor not to bother with the primary text of *The Romance of the Rose*, since Lewis's version was so much better![2] Although Lewis appealed to very different audiences with his work as a literary historian and critic, on the one hand, and with his imaginative fiction, on the other, there are some fascinating connections running between the different kinds of writing he practised.

One such connection is the concept of allegory, which was central both to the theory and the practice of Lewis's work as critic, and also to the theory and practice of his work as a writer of imaginative fiction. Towards the beginning of *The Allegory of Love* he offers a definition of allegory:

> On the one hand you start with an immaterial fact, such as the passions which you actually experience, and can then invent *visibilia* [visible entities] to express them. If you are hesitating between an angry retort and a soft answer, you can express your state of mind by inventing a person called *Ira* [Anger] with a torch and letting her contend with another invented person called *Patientia* [Patience]. This is allegory, and it is with this alone that we have to deal. (*AOL* 44–5)

This very precise and rather restrictive definition of allegory is sharply contrasted with another way of the relating the material to the immaterial, or the visible to the invisible:

> But there is another way... which is almost the opposite of allegory, and which I would call sacramentalism or symbolism. If our passions, being immaterial, can be copied by material inventions, then it is possible that our material world in its turn is the copy of an invisible world. The attempt to read [that invisible world] through its sensible [=perceptible by the senses] imitations, to see the archetype in the copy, is what I mean by symbolism... The allegorist leaves the given – his own passions – to talk of that which is confessedly less real, which is a fiction. The symbolist leaves the given to find another that is more real. To put the difference in another way, for the symbolist it is we who are the allegory. (*AOL* 45)

This concept of symbolism, whose difference from allegory 'can hardly be exaggerated', Lewis says, 'makes its first effective appearance in European thought with the dialogues of Plato' (*AOL* 45). It finds its greatest expression, however, in the time of the Romantics, and this, Lewis suggests, 'is significant of the profound difference that separates it from allegory (*AOL* 46). Lewis does not elaborate on why the connection with Romanticism should be significant, yet it is important to make explicit what Lewis leaves implicit. This is because Lewis's whole working definition of allegory, which opposes it sharply to symbol, is derived somewhat uncritically from the negative definition of allegory found in Romanticism in general and Coleridge in particular. The Romantic privileging of the vibrant, revelatory symbol over sterile and pedantic allegory was a not unjustified reaction to what allegory had become by the eighteenth century. But ironically the very allegories which Lewis was approaching in terms of this unsympathetic Romantic definition of allegory gave the lie to that definition. There is thus a fundamental inconsistency in *The Allegory of Love* between the restrictive definition of allegory to which Lewis is theoretically committed, and his actual practice as reader and critic of medieval allegory.

Lewis's theoretical commitment to the Romantic concept of allegory is not loud but deep. 'Symbolism', he says, 'is a mode of thought, but allegory is a mode of expression. It belongs to the form of poetry, more than to its content' (*AOL* 48). This idea is further examined in a paper on metaphor which Lewis gave not long after the publication of *The Allegory of Love*. 'Bluspels and Flalansferes: A Semantic Nightmare' is an essay whose strange title derives from Lewis's defamiliarizing tactic of inventing words to illustrate his discussion of 'dead' metaphors. The essay distinguishes between what Lewis calls 'the Master's metaphor' and 'the Pupil's metaphor'. Of these, he says:

> The first is freely chosen; it is one among many possible modes of expression; it does not at all hinder, and only very slightly helps, the thought of its maker. The second is not chosen at all; it is the unique expression of a meaning that we cannot have on any other terms; it dominates completely the thought of the recipient; his truth cannot rise above the truth of the original metaphor. (*SLE* 255)

This theory of the role of metaphor in language (which owes much to Owen Barfield's *Poetic Diction*) echoes the Romantic binary opposition between allegory and symbol. But the argument of the essay runs at the end into a kind of impasse, when Lewis writes:

> all our truth, or all but a few fragments, is won by metaphor. And thence, I confess, it does follow that if our thinking is ever true, then the metaphors by which we think must have been good metaphors. It does follow that if those original equations, between good and light, or evil and dark, between breath and soul and all the others, were from the beginning arbitrary and fanciful... then all our thinking is nonsensical. But we cannot, without contradiction, believe it to be nonsensical. And so, admittedly the view I have taken has metaphysical implications. But so has every other view. (*SLE* 265)

Lewis is caught here between, on the one hand, the recognition that, if language is fundamentally metaphorical, then any 'truth' that escapes the abyss of arbitrariness could only ever be imaginatively and aesthetically intuited, but not intellectually known (the 'Romantic' view); and, on the other hand, the 'rationalist' demand (with which he has just aligned himself) for intellectual certainty. In other words, Lewis is caught between 'Myth' (as he increasingly began to call symbolism) and 'Fact'.

Before Lewis the critic published *The Allegory of Love*, Lewis the creative writer had already published an allegory, *The Pilgrim's Regress: An Allegorical Apology for Christianity, Reason and Romanticism*. This was very much an allegory as subsequently defined in *The Allegory of Love*: 'the allegorist [in this case Lewis] leaves the given [his intellectual and religious development] to talk of that which is confessedly less real, which is a fiction' (*AOL* 45). The story is filled with amusing personifications; for example, Mr Halfways stands for Romanticism, Gus Halfways for Modernism, Sigismund Enlightenment for Freudianism, Mr Sensible for 'dilettante scepticism', and so on. Lewis felt compelled in later editions of the book to add a running headline to explain what the characters and story represented, just in case the reader failed to get the point. But, as Lewis showed himself aware in the Preface to the third edition of the book, the need for the headlines is in inverse proportion to the success of the work *as a story*. As he puts it: 'when allegory is at its best, it approaches myth [= symbolism, in *The Allegory of Love* terms], which must be grasped with the imagination, not with the intellect' (*PR* 19). It seems that Lewis is working with such an impoverished concept of allegory that, for an allegory to succeed as a story, it must turn into that which is defined as being its opposite – that is, myth or symbolism. If Lewis's own allegory does indeed fail *as a story*, the allegories he is dealing with in *The Allegory of Love* do strike us, largely through Lewis's skilful and enthusiastic advocacy, as interesting stories; that is to say, Lewis's defence of allegory only succeeds by pulling the texts he is defending away from the definition he has given for them.

One way of dealing with this inconsistency is to supply another category between Lewis's leaky vessels of allegory and myth/symbolism. Paul Piehler has suggested a distinction between what he calls 'the allegory of vision' and its poor cousin, 'the allegory of demystification'.[3] The latter category, classically represented by Prudentius' depiction in *Psychomachia* of a battle between personified Virtues and Vices, was, according to Lewis, originally a way of dealing with, by bringing to representation, forces which we would now call 'unconscious'. This kind of allegory as 'psychic defence by personification' outlived its usefulness, and by the eighteenth century had degenerated into the 'frigid personifications' rightly criticized by the Romantics. It is also the concept of allegory that Lewis was working with in *The Allegory of Love,* and it does not fit the medieval allegories he was mostly writing about. Rather than abandon the concept of allegory altogether, Piehler suggests a new concept of allegory, 'the allegory of vision', which fits much better the material Lewis was actually dealing with. It also fits the imaginative fiction Lewis himself was later to write, after his relatively unsuccessful attempt at an 'allegory of demystification' in *The Pilgrim's Regress.*

Whether or not one accepts Piehler's label of 'allegory of vision' for this 'other' kind of allegory which resists Lewis's narrowly prescriptive definition, one can see this 'other' 'other-speak' (the literal meaning of the Greek word *allegoria*) taking shape between the lines of *The Allegory of Love.* What emerges is something which not only looks like what Lewis will describe as the second kind of Romanticism in his list of Romanticisms in the Preface to *The Pilgrim's Regress;* it also looks like what Lewis himself will write in his science-fiction trilogy and in the Narnia books. Of his Romanticism no. 2 Lewis says: 'The marvellous is "romantic", provided it does not make part of the believed religion' (*PR* 10). In *The Allegory of Love* Lewis claims, while discussing Prudentius' contemporary Claudian, that:

> the decline of the gods, from deity to hypostasis [a personified attribute of God], and from hypostasis to decoration, was not, for them or for us, a history of sheer loss. For decoration may let romance in. The poet is free to invent, beyond the limit of the possible, regions of strangeness and beauty for their own sake. I do not mean, necessarily, that Claudian is a romantic.... [But] under the pretext of allegory something else has slipped in ... something which, under many names, lurks at the back of most romantic poetry. I mean the 'other world' not of religion, but of imagination; the land of longing, the Earthly Paradise, the garden east of the sun and west of the moon. (*AOL* 75–6)

As Lewis sums up: 'we see the beginnings of that free creation of the marvellous which first slips in under the cloak of allegory. ... For poetry to spread its wings fully, there must be, besides the believed religion, a marvellous that knows itself as myth' (*AOL*

82–3). Lewis could easily be talking about his own imaginative writing, and its ambiguous relation to allegory. Indeed later in *The Allegory Of Love*, in a phrase which might be the best short description of his own creative writing, he describes the work of Chrétien de Troyes as 'mere romantic supposals' ('mere' in Lewis needs always to be taken with a grain of salt!).

MERE ROMANTIC SUPPOSALS

Lewis always denied *The Chronicles of Narnia* and his science-fiction trilogy were allegorical, to the puzzlement of many readers who felt instinctively that they were. His denial rests on the narrow definition of allegory made in *The Allegory of Love*, as is clear in the following extract from a letter written in 1958:

> By allegory I mean a composition . . . in which immaterial realities are represented by feigned physical objects; e.g. a pictured Cupid allegorically represents erotic love . . . or, in Bunyan, a giant represents Despair. . . . If Aslan represented the immaterial Deity in the same way in which Giant Despair represented Despair, he would be an allegorical figure. (*L*. 475)

But the idea that he 'drew up a list of basic Christian truths and hammered out "allegories" to embody them . . . is all pure moonshine', Lewis says (*OTOW* 72). For Lewis, Aslan is not an allegorical figure at all; rather he is what Lewis called a *supposal*, that is:

> an invention giving an imaginary answer to the question, 'What might Christ become like, if there really were a world like Narnia and He chose to be incarnate and die and rise again in that world as He actually has done in ours?' This is not allegory at all. So in *Perelandra* [the second of Lewis's science-fiction trilogy]. This also works out a *supposition*. (*L*. 475, emphasis in original)

Lewis often reiterated in almost identical terms this insistence that the Narnia books and the science-fiction trilogy were not allegories but supposals. A crucial difference between allegory and supposals is that:

> they mix the real and the unreal in different ways. Bunyan's picture of Giant Despair does not start from a supposal at all. It is not a supposition but a *fact* that despair can capture and imprison the

> human soul. What is unreal (fictional) is the giant, the castle, and the dungeon. The incarnation of Christ in another world is a mere supposal; but *granted* the supposition, He really would have been a physical object in that world. (*L*. 475–6, emphasis in original)

This attempt by Lewis to establish a clear division between 'fact' and 'fiction' is related to his similar attempt to divide 'literal' from 'metaphorical' language in his essay 'Bluspels and Flalansferes'. Allegory is the merely fictional decoration of statements of fact whose truth may be legitimated by reason alone; 'supposal' (or myth, which is the real 'other' of allegory), which *in principle* differs from any kind of factual truth, can only be 'received' in an 'imaginative embrace'. This phrase comes from Lewis's essay 'Myth Became Fact' (*U*. 42), where he seeks sharply to demarcate two modes of apprehension – abstract intellectual understanding versus concrete imaginative experience ('knowing' versus 'tasting') – only in order to claim that they are paradoxically united in our response to the unique event of the Incarnation in which 'Myth became Fact'. This idea was central to Lewis's conversion to orthodox Christian faith. It was the momentous discussion with Tolkien and Hugo Dyson in 1931 which helped him to move from a merely intellectual assent to an abstract theism to a faith which was *both* an assent to real historical Fact *and* an 'imaginative embrace' of a Myth which loses none of its 'mythical radiance' for being also Fact – 'Christ is *more* than Balder, not less' as Lewis puts it (*U*. 43).

Whatever the theological implications of Lewis's particular 'take' on Christology may be, the implications for the practice of creative writing are considerable. If, as Lewis says, 'God chooses to be mythopoeic', this means not only that Christians should be '*mythopathic*' (*U*. 43, emphasis in original) – that is, willing imaginatively to embrace myth; it also legitimates and actually encourages appropriately gifted Christians to *practise* the art of myth-making. This fundamentally Romantic idea came to Lewis from German Romanticism, particularly from Novalis, via George MacDonald; and more directly from Owen Barfield's interpretation of Coleridge. Barfield also influenced Tolkien's theory of 'sub-creation', to which Lewis subscribed. Tolkien's theory is set out in his poem 'Mythopeia', which was generated in part by that crucial discussion with Lewis and Dyson in 1931. A key passage in the poem runs:

> Man, Sub-creator, the refracted Light
> through whom is splintered from a single White
> to many hues, and endlessly combined
> in living shapes that move from mind to mind.[4]

In the Epilogue to the essay 'On Fairy-Stories', Tolkien connects such sub-creation with 'joy', which he says is 'the mark of the true fairy-story (or romance)'. He continues:

> Probably every writer making a secondary world, a fantasy, every sub-creator, wishes in some measure to be a real maker, or hopes that... the peculiar quality of this secondary world... is derived from Reality.... If he indeed achieves a quality... [of] 'inner consistency of reality', it is difficult to see how this can be, if the work does not in some way partake of reality. The peculiar quality of the 'joy' in successful Fantasy can thus be explained as a sudden glimpse of the underlying reality or truth.[5]

One of the effects of the regular exchange of ideas among 'the Inklings' (the circle of friends – almost a writers' workshop – at Oxford, whose number included Lewis, Tolkien, Barfield, and Charles Williams) was that their ideas 'interpenetrated' to a great extent. Thus something written by one of them (in this case, by Tolkien) can apply remarkably well to the work of another (in this case Lewis). What Tolkien says about sub-creation pulls together Lewis's ideas about the 'mythical radiance' of mere supposals, whose power derives in part from the fact that they are *not* believed ('the gods must be disinfected of belief...before that other divinity can come to light in the imagination' (*AOL* 83)); and the Joy which, as Lewis amply illustrates in *Surprised by Joy*, is a *tasting*, if not a knowing, of reality. In a deeply Romantic gesture, Lewis thus *aestheticizes* 'truth'. In his middle years Lewis's commitment to communicating his Christian faith 'in pictures' (in myths and 'mere supposals', and *not* in allegories as he defined them) went in tandem with an equal commitment to communicating that faith by rational argument. How what was in tandem came to be in tension will be discussed below. For the moment let us turn to the first sequence of 'pictures' in which Lewis offers us 'a marvellous that knows itself as myth' (*AOL* 83) – the science-fiction trilogy.

REGIONS OF STRANGENESS AND BEAUTY

While it is possible to see the genre of Lewis's science-fiction trilogy (*Out of the Silent Planet*, *Perelandra* (also called *Voyage to Venus*), and *That Hideous Strength*) taking shape between the lines of *The Allegory of Love*, it has also to be said that the trilogy transgresses any established definitions of genre. Although the young Lewis had what he calls a 'ravenous lust' for the 'scientifiction' of writers such as H. G. Wells, this had little to do with any 'romantic spell' or Joy (*SBJ* 34). His own 'planetary romances', he says, were not so much the gratification as the 'exorcism' of that 'peculiar, heady attraction' for other planets (*SBJ* 34). The exorcism worked by reconciling the 'coarse strength' of this 'fierce curiosity' with 'the more elusive, and genuinely imaginative, impulse' (*SBJ* 34). Such a transformation of science fiction into a new literary genre, which could carry a *spiritual* weight, originates not with Lewis himself but with David Lindsay, the author of the flawed but startlingly original *Voyage to Arcturus* (1920). Lewis says in a letter that he first learned from Lindsay that other planets in fiction are good for *spiritual* adventures. They can satisfy 'the craving that sends our imaginations off the earth'. In Lindsay he saw 'the terrific results' produced by combining two kinds of fiction hitherto kept apart – 'the Novalis, G. MacDonald sort' and 'the H. G. Wells, Jules Verne sort'.[6] This Novalis–MacDonald tradition is clearly identifiable with 'the marvellous that knows itself as myth'. Unlike other kinds of science fiction, it is unconcerned about technological plausibility. As Lewis puts it in the same essay, referring to the journeys to Mars in *Out of the Silent Planet* and to Venus in *Perelandra*: 'I took a hero once to Mars in a space-ship, but when I knew better I had angels convey him to Venus. Nor need the strange worlds, when we get there, be at all strictly tied to scientific probabilities. It is their wonder, or beauty, or suggestiveness that matters' (*OTOW* 91).

Although the mode of transportation, and indeed the central issue, in *Out of the Silent Planet* is dependent on the existence of modern scientific research, nevertheless even in the first of the science-fiction trilogy Lewis is at least as interested in the medieval past as he is in any technological future. There is a sense in which *Out of the Silent Planet* originates in appendix I of

The Allegory of Love, where Lewis discusses the term *Oyarses* used by the medieval Platonist Bernardus Sylvestris. Lewis refers to the advice given him on this subject by Professor C. C. J. Webb. In chapter XXII of *Out of the Silent Planet*, where the narrator explains how he came to be writing up Ransom's adventures on Mars (or 'Malacandra'), he quotes a paragraph from a letter he once wrote to Ransom; the paragraph is almost identical to the relevant paragraph in *The Allegory of Love*, even including a reference to 'C.J.'. It was the narrator's passing reference to the term *Oyarses*, so strikingly similar to *Oyarsa*, the word in 'Old Solar' for the ruling spirit of a planet, which prompted Ransom to tell the narrator about his adventures on Malacandra, which he had hitherto kept secret. Apart from the self-referential game Lewis is playing, the reference to Bernardus Sylvestris illustrates how much Lewis drew his inspiration for *Out of the Silent Planet* from his reading of medieval literature, where we find, as he says, 'the beginnings of that free invention of the marvellous' with its 'regions of strangeness and beauty' (*AOL* 82, 75).

If the narrator of *Out of the Silent Planet* and *Perelandra* is obviously 'Lewis', there is some critical discussion of who Ransom is. The fact that Ransom is a philologist has led some readers to assume that he is based on Tolkien. Tolkien himself was of the opinion that he 'may have had some part in him [Ransom]';[7] on the other hand, there is a purely functional motivation for making Ransom a philologist so that he can rapidly acquire 'Old Solar', the language spoken on Malacandra and Perelandra. Other factors suggest that, at least in the first two books of the trilogy, Ransom is based on Lewis himself as much as on anyone else (in *That Hideous Strength* Ransom strikingly resembles Lewis's friend Charles Williams). Despite such speculation about the 'identity' of Ransom, he is referred to in the first paragraph of *Out of the Silent Planet* simply as 'the Pedestrian'. Besides hinting at *Pilgrim's Progress*, this unusual way of introducing Ransom, a Cambridge don on a walking holiday, emphasizes the ordinariness of the protagonist who is about to undergo the most extraordinary adventures. The first two chapters see Ransom kidnapped by Devine, an unscrupulous entrepreneur, and Weston, the archetypal mad scientist, who need an earthling to take to the *sorns* of Malacandra. Devine and Weston, for whom the inhabitants of Malacandra are merely savages, assume that they want a human for some kind of sacrifice, and it is for this purpose that they have brought Ransom. In fact they have misinterpreted the message from the Oyarsa of Malacandra who had merely wished a Thulcandrian (an earthling) to be brought to him to inform him about 'Maleldil's [Christ's] strange wars there [on Thulcandra or Earth] with the Bent one [Satan]' (*CT* 109). Thulcandra is the eponymous 'Silent Planet' because after its Oyarsa (Lucifer) had become 'bent', and had almost destroyed Malacandra, he was banned from 'the Heavens' and confined to Thulcandra, with which all contact has been lost. Thus elements of Christian 'salvation history' have been transposed into a different mythological frame as 'mere supposals'.

The Oyarsa of Malacandra also wants to know why the Thulcandrians Weston and Devine turned up on his planet in the first place. For Devine the only motivation, Ransom tells the Oyarsa, is 'the sun's blood' (gold). Weston's motivation is less crude. 'Westonism', as Lewis elsewhere calls it, is the theory that the development of human technology would allow humans to colonize other planets, and so to live forever as 'they leap from world to world . . . always going to a new sun when an old one dies' (*CT* 110). Lewis told one of his correspondents that what set him about writing *Out of the Silent Planet* 'was the discovery that a pupil of mine took all that dream of interplanetary colonization quite seriously, and the realization that thousands of people in one way or another depend on some hope of perpetuating and improving the human race for the whole meaning of the universe – that a "scientific" hope of defeating death is a real rival to Christianity' (*L.* 321). *Out of the Silent Planet* is, therefore, a kind of counter-propaganda. As Lewis puts it in another letter:

> What immediately spurred me to write [*OSP*] was Olaf Stapledon's *Last and First Men* and an essay in J. B. S. Haldane's *Possible Worlds*, both of which seemed to take the idea of such travel seriously and to have the desperately immoral outlook I try to pillory in Weston. I like the whole inter-planetary idea as a *mythology* and simply wished to conquer for my own (Christian) point of view what has always hitherto been used by the opposite side.[8]

The fact that Lewis chose to oppose 'Westonism' with *myth* is significant, for, while he was quite willing at this period of his life to use rational arguments against the likes of 'Westonism', he was equally ready to deploy the power of myth in defence of Christianity. As was noted above in relation to his essay 'Myth Became Fact', Lewis contrasted intellectual knowing with imaginative 'tasting'. What is most striking about *Out of the Silent Planet* is the way Lewis manages to let the reader 'taste' and 'feel' the beauty of the Heavens, and of Malacandra, in a way which reveals the poverty of Weston's desiccated world-view. Ransom's first numinous experience comes on the voyage to Malacandra. Of Ransom's 'exultation of heart' Lewis writes:

> A nightmare, long engendered in the modern mind by the mythology that follows in the wake of science, was falling off him. He had read of 'Space': at the back of his thinking for years had lurked the dismal fancy of the black, cold vacuity, the utter deadness, which was supposed to separate the worlds.... now that very name 'Space' seemed a blasphemous libel for this empyrean ocean of radiance in which they swam. He could not call it 'dead'; he felt life pouring into him at every moment. How indeed could it be otherwise, since out of this ocean the worlds and all their life had come? He had thought it barren; he saw now that it was the womb of worlds, whose blazing and innumerable offspring looked down nightly upon the Earth . . . No: Space was the wrong name. Older thinkers had been wiser when they named it simply the heavens – the heavens which declared the glory – the
>
> 'happy climes that ly
> Where day never shuts his eye
> Up in the broad fields of the sky.'
>
> He quoted Milton's words to himself lovingly, at this time and often. (*CT* 26–7)

'Older thinkers had been wiser' is a typical Lewis comment. More specifically, as he argues in *The Discarded Image*: 'Nothing is more deeply impressed on the cosmic imaginings of a modern than the idea that the heavenly bodies move in a pitch-black and dead-cold vacuity. It was not so in the Medieval Model' (*DI* 111). Although Ransom quotes Milton, 'Milton here is medieval', as Lewis puts it when quoting the same lines in his essay 'Imagination and Thought in the Middle Ages' (*SMRL* 53).

But it is the sheer strangeness and beauty of Malacandra, so powerfully evoked by Lewis, that remain with the reader. In a Postscript to the book, 'Dr Ransom' responds to the narrator's attempts to portray Ransom's adventures; he admits he is disappointed. For example, he writes:

> How can one 'get across' the Malacandrian *smells*? Nothing comes back to me more vividly in my dreams... especially the early morning smell in those purple woods, where the very mention of 'early morning' and 'woods' is misleading because it must set you thinking of... the smell of our own planet, but I'm thinking of something totally different. More 'aromatic'... yes, but then it is not hot or luxurious or exotic as that word suggests. Something aromatic, spicy, yet very cold, very thin, tingling at the back of the nose – something that did to the sense of smell what high, sharp violin notes do to the ear.... I am homesick for my old Malacandrian valley when I think of it. (*CT* 139)

Later in *Perelandra* Ransom will make the same paradoxical comment about being homesick for another planet. But such homesickness goes much further back than any visit to any planet. It is, of course, 'Sweet Desire' itself, the Desire which was at the core of Lewis's being. As Lewis puts it in *Perelandra*:

> It was strange to be filled with homesickness for places where his sojourn had been so brief and which were... so alien to our race. Or were they? A cord of longing which drew him to the invisible isle seemed to him at that moment to have been fastened long, long before his coming to Perelandra, long before the earliest times that memory could recover in his childhood, before his birth, before the birth of man himself, before the origins of time. It was sharp, sweet, wild, and holy, all in one... (*CT* 235)

As a mythical embodiment of 'the land of longing, the Earthly Paradise' (*AOL* 75), *Perelandra* is for many readers, including Lewis himself, one of his greatest literary achievements. Elements of the traditional science-fiction story, such as the spaceship, and some degree of suspense, did feature in *Out of the Silent Planet*, but they are practically absent from *Perelandra* (only the final struggle with the 'Un-man', as the devil-possessed Weston is called, has an element of suspense). The book is in part a prose-poem, in part a philosophical dialogue, and in part, as Lewis himself pointed out, a kind of opera (*L.* 375). After an introductory section in which 'Lewis' has to fight his way past Thulcandra's 'bent eldila' (Earth's fallen angels) to reach Ransom's cottage, Ransom is transported in a 'celestial coffin' to Perelandra. The planet is mostly covered in water, apart from one area of 'Fixed Land', and some floating islands. It was

Lewis's mental picture of these floating islands which was the starting point for *Perelandra* (*OTOW* 181). Elsewhere Lewis says: 'All my Narnia books and my three science fiction books began with seeing pictures in my head. At first they were not a story, just pictures' (*OTOW* 79). The picture of floating islands, probably derived from Olaf Stapledon's book mentioned above,[9] was developed into a story about 'an averted fall' (*OTOW* 181). Around the time Lewis was writing *Perelandra* he was also giving lectures on Milton's *Paradise Lost*, published as *A Preface to 'Paradise Lost'* in 1942, a year before the publication of *Perelandra*. Lewis says in a letter that *Perelandra*, like the Narnia books, 'works out a *supposition*. ("Suppose even now, in some other planet there were a first couple undergoing the same that Adam and Eve underwent here, but successfully")' (*L.* 375). In the Perelandrian version of the Fall story, the tempter is Weston, who has been led to the planet for this purpose. In fact it is never quite clear to what extent the spirit animating Weston's body is actually Weston, or Satan himself who, in a dramatic transformation scene reminiscent of film versions of *Dr Jekyll and Mr Hyde*, enters into Weston's body at the scientist's own invitation. One of the genuinely eerie elements in the book is the uncertainty as to whether it is Weston speaking through the mouth of 'the Un-man', or Satan himself. Prior to Weston's possession by Satan, it had been apparent in his dialogue with Ransom that he had progressed beyond 'mere Westonism'. The goal of interplanetary colonization has in principle been achieved. During his convalescence after the Malacandrian episode, Weston has developed an interest in 'spirituality' (*CT* 225–7). He preaches to Ransom a doctrine of 'emergent evolution', a mishmash of Life-philosophies with echoes of Bergson, Nietzsche, and Hegel, culminating in the cry: 'I *am* the Universe. I, Weston, am your God and your Devil. I call that Force into me completely...' (*CT* 230).

But even in this first encounter between Ransom and Weston, some of the technical problems relating to the book's form begin to emerge. Early in the dialogue Ransom is 'filled with a sense of crazy irrelevance' and reflects: 'Here were two human beings, thrown together in an alien world under conditions of inconceivable strangeness... Was it sane – was it imaginable – that they should find themselves at once engaged in a philosophical argument which might just as well have occurred in a Cambridge combination room?' (*CT* 223). The fact that Lewis admits that there is a kind of craziness about his whole scenario does not help to make it more credible. This, and subsequent dialogues, however interesting they may be philosophically, sometimes *do* seem incongruous, and sometimes *are* frankly unimaginable. Such incongruity is a result of Lewis failing to balance two very different impulses: on the one hand, Lewis the philosopher wants to argue rationally; on the other hand, Lewis the poet is committed to the power of myth and the Romantic imagination. Lewis's books of the 1930s and 1940s are dominated by this tension. Some books, such as *Out of the Silent Planet*, tend very much towards the 'myth' pole; others, such as the apologetic writing, seek to convince by rational argument. Much of Lewis's writing falls somewhere between the two poles, and is a mixture of both. *The Screwtape Letters* and *The Great Divorce* present highly imaginative settings for discussion of religious issues; but only the latter book contains genuinely mythical elements. *Perelandra* is an at times uneasy mixture of myth and philosophical discussion – as, for example, when Ransom and Weston engage in an extended discussion of death and nihilism while riding on dolphin-like fish over the Perelandrian ocean.

Nevertheless there are in *Perelandra* powerful elements of pure myth on which the philosophical and theological discussions are superimposed. Lewis several times presents the idea that 'what was myth in one world might always be fact in some other' (*CT* 235). What prompts this thought is Ransom's encounter with mermen and mermaids. Earlier in his sojourn on Perelandra Ransom had awakened to find that something was happening to him 'which perhaps never happens to a man until he is out of his own world: he saw reality and it was a dream. He opened his eyes and saw a strange heraldically coloured tree loaded with yellow fruits and silver leaves. Round the base of the indigo stem was coiled a small dragon covered with scales of red gold. He recognized the garden of the Hesperides at once' (*CT* 182). Ransom not only feels that he is living – quite literally – 'in Paradise' (*CT* 281); he also has the sensation 'not of following an adventure, but of enacting a myth' (*CT* 185). The distinction between fact and myth is, he concludes, 'purely terrestrial' (*CT* 277); it is the result of the Fall, and so, Ransom discovers, applies only on Earth:

> Long since on Mars, and more strongly since he came to Perelandra, Ransom had been perceiving that the triple distinction of truth from myth and of both from fact was purely terrestrial – was part and parcel of that unhappy division between soul and body which resulted from the Fall. . . . The Incarnation had been the beginning of its disappearance. In Perelandra it would have no meaning at all. Whatever happened here would be of such a nature that Earth-men would call it mythological. All this he had thought before. Now he knew it. (*CT* 273–4)

The distinction between 'knowing' and 'tasting' made in 'Myth Became Fact', published a year after *Perelandra*, is overcome on Earth only by the Incarnation, Lewis says. But on Perelandra it literally does not apply, as the narrator points out when Ransom eats some seaweed on one of his Perelandrian fish-rides: 'while Ransom was on Perelandra his sense of taste had become something more than it was on Earth: it gave knowledge as well as pleasure, though not a knowledge that can be reduced to words' (*CT* 291).

Such a collapsing or overcoming of the distinction between myth and fact is a bold gesture on Lewis's part, both in theological and literary terms. In theological terms, while every attempt is made in *Perelandra* to emphasize the central place of the Incarnation in cosmic history, there is a strong speculative interest in alternative scenarios where an Incarnation is not necessary, because a Fall has not occurred. It is ironical that a writer so venerated by the orthodox could be accused of a kind of presumption in seeking to join together in his fiction the 'myth' and 'fact' that Lewis elsewhere says could only be reconciled by the Incarnation. Is there a possibility here of Lewis's mythopoeic powers being set (unconsciously, no doubt) alongside the mythopoeic powers of God? One way of reading Lewis (again an irony, given Lewis's ultra-orthodox reputation) is as a kind of modern Christian Gnostic, developing his own speculative mythology which is founded on, but goes far beyond, the orthodox Christian story. Lewis has often been called a Christian Platonist; but history tells us that the dividing line between Platonism and Gnosticism is far less clear than the orthodox would wish. The tradition in which Lewis stands goes back from Barfield through MacDonald, Novalis, and Coleridge, to the Renaissance and Medieval Platonists, and all the way back to Origen and the early Christian Platonists; it has always had strong Gnostic tendencies and therefore an uneasy relationship with Christian orthodoxy. It may be no accident that 'archons', the mighty rulers who are standard features of Gnostic mythology, should appear in the penultimate chapter of *Perelandra*. As we will see below, Lewis strove in his apologetic writings to be an uncompromisingly orthodox Christian; but perhaps Lewis the Christian apologist stands in some tension with Lewis the inveterate myth-maker, the sub-creator who seems to have some problems with the 'sub'!

The difficulty that Lewis, in contrast with Tolkien, faces with his mythical sub-creation is that it is not kept completely separate from the religion that is believed as fact. The kind of 'marvellous that knows itself as myth' which Lewis created needs to be 'disinfected of belief'; it has to be based on 'the old marvellous which was once taken as fact' – but no longer so (*AOL* 83). The '"other world" not of religion but of imagination', 'the regions of strangeness and beauty' (*AOL* 75), depend on the decline of belief in the elements that comprise them. But in the science-fiction trilogy, and especially in *Perelandra*, Lewis does mix 'mere romantic supposals' with myth that *is* believed as fact. This confers on Lewis's myth, and specifically on his hero Ransom, a status which should make orthodox Christians uncomfortable. On the other hand, Christians who find the Gnostic tradition enriching rather than threatening can readily embrace the myths Lewis creates in the science-fiction trilogy; they will find little that is not also to be found in Novalis or in George MacDonald. Readers for whom the Christian God is as dead as the gods of the ancient world may enjoy Lewis's myths in the exactly same way that Lewis himself enjoyed the romantic marvellous he described in *The Allegory of Love*.

The obliteration of the distinction between 'myth' and 'fact' can present problems not only for the orthodox Christian reader, but also for the politically motivated 'suspicious' reader, who will tend to see Lewis's writing as a prime example of 'Romantic ideology'. From such a critical perspective it is obvious that Lewis *would* want to show unpalatable (to Lewis) political 'facts' transfigured by consoling (to Lewis) 'myths'. The overcoming of the 'fallen', terrestrial distinction between fact and myth, between literal and metaphorical uses of language, could be seen as just another version of the old Romantic nostalgia for an 'organic unity' which falsifies the actual divisions of experience.

To make matters worse, the mythological vision presented by Lewis is unashamedly hierarchical (democracy was for Lewis only a regrettable necessity in a fallen world). It is also deeply essentialist, not least in relation to gender. In a remarkable passage which becomes all the more striking in the light of later developments in feminist criticism (at which Lewis could hardly have guessed), Ransom encounters 'the real meaning of gender' (*CT* 327). Gender is not, we are told, 'an imaginative extension of sex'; on the contrary, 'Gender is a reality, and a more fundamental reality than sex. Sex is . . . merely the adaptation to organic life of a fundamental polarity which divides all created beings. Female sex is simply one of the things that have feminine gender; there are many others, and Masculine and Feminine meet us on planes of reality where male and female would be simply meaningless' (*CT* 327). Ransom sees the reality of gender displayed in the descent to a mountain peak in Perelandra of the Oyeresu (or archons) of Malacandra and Perelandra (Mars and Venus, in terms of earthly mythology):

> All this Ransom saw, as it were, with his own eyes. The two white creatures were sexless. But he of Malacandra was masculine (not male); she of Perelandra was feminine (not female). Malacandra seemed to him to have the look of one standing armed, at the ramparts of his own remote archaic world, in ceaseless vigilance, his eyes ever roaming the earthward horizon whence his danger came long ago. 'A sailor's look,' Ransom once said to me; 'you know . . . eyes that are impregnated with distance.' But the eyes of Perelandra opened, as it were, inward, as if they were the curtained gateway to a world of caves and murmurings and wandering airs, of life that rocked in winds and splashed on mossy stones and descended as the dew and arose sunward in thin-spun delicacy of mist. On Mars the very forests are of stone; in Venus the lands swim. (*CT* 327–8)

Now we know what archons (as well as little girls and little boys) are made of!

The above passage almost seems written to exemplify the 'dual, *hierarchized* oppositions' Hélène Cixous describes in her famous essay 'Sorties'. All that can be said is that Lewis's adherence to what Cixous calls 'the Old order' is entirely explicit; indeed the existing order is not nearly old enough for Lewis. The order he longs for is not obviously identifiable with any power structure in the modern world. His 'discarded image' or world-view is medieval, essentialist, and hierarchical, but by no means rigid; it is Platonist, but draws on that current in the Platonic (and especially the Neo-platonic) tradition which is open to the *play* of the complex and differentiated structure of reality. This vision is expressed above all in the operatic conclusion of *Perelandra*, where the eldila (angels) sing the praises of the Great Game, or Great Dance. The Great Dance is certainly hierarchical: 'All is righteousness and there is no equality. Not as when stones lie side by side, but as when stones support and are supported in an arch, such is his order' (*CT* 340–1). On the other hand, the very dust itself: 'which is scattered so rare in Heaven . . . is at the centre. . . . [A]s sparks fly out of a fire, He utters in each grain of it the unmixed image of his energy. Each grain, if it spoke, would say, I am the centre; for me all things were made' (*CT* 342). The plan of the Great Game is so grand that it escapes the human mind:

> All that is made seems planless to the darkened mind, because there are more plans than it looked for. In these seas [of Perelandra] there are islands where the hairs of the turf are so fine and so closely woven that unless a man looked long at them he would see neither hairs nor weaving at all, but only the same and the flat. So with the Great Dance. Set your eyes on one movement and it will lead you through all patterns and it will seem to you the master movement. But the seeming will be true. . . . There seems no plan because all is plan; there seems no centre because it is all centre. (*CT* 344)

Many such passages in this hymn of praise could be compared with similar passages in Plotinus, the great Neo-platonist philosopher. The conclusion too resembles Plotinus, though with its talk of 'the Abyss' it also seems to be drifting into the company of Valentinus, a Christian contemporary of Plotinus, whom the Church ultimately decided was a Gnostic heretic:

> Yet this seeming also is the end and final cause for which He spreads out Time so long and Heaven so deep; lest if we never met the dark, and the road that leads no-whither, and the question to which no answer is imaginable, we should have in our minds no likeness of the Abyss of the Father, into which if a creature drop down his

thoughts for ever he shall hear no echo return to him. (*CT* 344)

If such a negative theology is reminiscent of certain passages in some modern thinkers such as Heidegger and Derrida, that is because these thinkers are consciously playing with motifs from the Christian mystical tradition. While Lewis can be an aggressively dogmatic Christian in the context of an argument, as a creator of myth his position is much more ambiguous, and he is willing to entertain imaginatively ideas which are on the margins of Christian orthodoxy.

Finally, it is worth underlining the importance in *Perelandra* of the contrast between free play and rigid structure. Satan in the form of Weston tempts the Green Lady (the Eve of Perelandra) to transgress Maleldil's command not to settle on the 'Fixed Land'. In a sense the whole point of this command is that it has no point, other than as an opportunity for obedience for its own sake. Similarly, according to Lewis in *A Preface to Paradise Lost*, the apple in the Garden of Eden has for Milton, who here follows Augustine, no *intrinsic* importance (*PPL* 68–9). But the commandment not to settle on the Fixed Land is more than an empty rule, set just to make a theological point; it also has a symbolic resonance. Perhaps rather surprisingly, given Lewis's tendency to conservatism in religious matters, the stability of living on the Fixed Land is not what Maleldil has ordained for the inhabitants of Perelandra; rather they are to have a life on the open wave. Since the contours of the Perelandrian islands are constantly changing in response to the shape of the waves on which they float, life on the islands is literally 'going with the flow'. Symbolically there is a tension between the desire to be in control of one's own life, and a willingness to respond flexibly to whatever is sent by God. The idea of even wishing to be in control of one's experience comes as a shock to the Green Lady. One of the best things in *Perelandra* is Lewis's subtle psychological descriptions of the way in which the Lady gradually loses an innocence or immediacy of experience and begins to acquire self-consciousness and reflection – what she calls 'stepping out of life into the Alongside and looking at oneself living as if one were not alive' (*CT* 197). Although it was published after *Perelandra*, it is hard not to think of Lacan's famous essay on 'the mirror stage' when at a crucial moment Weston (or Satan) produces a mirror, and says to the Lady: 'Hold it further away and you will see the whole of the alongside woman – the other who is yourself' (*CT* 269). What Lewis seems to be after is a kind of fluid selfhood achieved by avoiding the Fall into a fixed, alienated self-consciousness. One is reminded of Kristeva's 'subject-in-process', which, by the power of 'the semiotic' (a pre-intellectual 'taste' of the real), can resist enclosure into 'the Symbolic order'. Thus Lewis's imaginative writing can have a power, and an engagement with contemporary theoretical concerns, which contrasts with the generally more limited appeal and relevance of his rather dated philosophical arguments.

The opposite, however, obtains in the case of *That Hideous Strength*, which is not only less successful than his two previous science-fiction books, but has also worn less well than the philosophical essay with which it is explicitly linked. In the Preface to *That Hideous Strength* Lewis writes that behind this '"tall story" about devilry' lies 'a serious "point" which I have tried to make in my *Abolition of Man*' (*CT* 353). The third volume of the science-fiction trilogy differs from the first two in several respects. Although it refers to Ransom's interplanetary travels, it does not itself portray a voyage to another planet. Lewis virtually abandons the science-fiction genre, and seems to switch to another genre altogether; the book is subtitled 'a modern fairy-tale for grown ups'. Its subtitle may be influenced by the subtitle of *Phantastes: A Faerie Romance for Men and Women* by George MacDonald, who is mentioned in Lewis's book, and an anthology of whose writing Lewis published a year after the publication of *That Hideous Strength*. But even *Phantastes* is about a journey to the other world of Fairyland (and indeed contains an account of 'a far-off planet'). The real model for *That Hideous Strength* is Charles Williams's 'supernatural thrillers' or 'spiritual shockers', where the supernatural intervenes dramatically into contemporary middle-class England. *That Hideous Strength* is on one level about the marital problems of Jane and Mark Studdock, resolved in the end by the influence of Ransom and his heavenly companions, the eldila. Jane is a doctoral student, working on Donne; Mark is a pushy sociology don, whose 'education had been neither scientific nor classical – merely "Modern". The severities both of abstraction and of high human tradition had passed him by... He was a man of straw, a glib examinee in subjects that require no exact knowledge...' (*CT*

540). He is drawn into the 'inner ring' (a term of contempt used by Lewis, who detested politically motivated cliques) first of his college, and subsequently of the newly established research centre of the National Institute of Co-ordinated Experiments (NICE). Mark embodies all that Lewis hated in the 'modern' education system which he attacked in *The Abolition of Man*. Lewis's main target in the latter is the influence on the study of English of the kind of philosophy which, like Logical Positivism, reduces all statements either to scientifically testable assertions of fact, or to merely emotive expressions of subjective preference. Objective value, which for Lewis is the condition of the possibility of being human, is abolished. Hence modern education is (usually unwittingly) 'the abolition of man'. Although Lewis could only have guessed at the later dominant influence in English Studies of the explicitly anti-humanistic varieties of poststructuralism, nevertheless his argument against the nihilism at the heart of a thoroughgoing relativism is, *mutatis mutandis*, relevant to contemporary debate. He insists on the primacy of tradition (or the 'Tao', as he calls it, to distance himself from the accusation of special Christian pleading) as the enabling medium of all human thought and value, and is deeply suspicious of the motivations of the project of modern scientific enquiry. Scientific endeavour is, he says, the twin of magical endeavour. One of these twins, magic (which, Lewis argues, was actually a sixteenth- and seventeenth-century phenomenon, rather than a medieval one) was sickly and died; nevertheless both twins were born of the same impulse – 'to subdue reality to the wishes of men', by means of 'technique' (*AOM* 46).

These ideas are embodied in *That Hideous Strength*. Mark's lack of what Lewis considered a proper education leaves him defenceless against the seductive power of the NICE, whose 'inner ring' is consciously nihilistic; its Deputy Director 'had passed from Hegel into Hume, thence through Pragmatism, and thence through Logical Positivism, and out at last into the complete void' (*CT* 721). Only the most inner ring of all knows that the 'Head' of the NICE, literally the head of the guillotined scientist Alcasan, is being kept alive not by the scientific apparatus attached to it, but by the powers of darkness, the 'Macrobes', as the bent eldils are called in this context. The NICE wants to revive Merlin to help them complete their project of world domination and the eventual – literal – abolition of man. But Merlin is recruited by the other side, the community headed by Ransom, now Mr Fisher-King, the Pendragon. Merlin reluctantly agrees to let the Oyeresu take possession of him, and thereby becomes the agent of the final cataclysm at a great banquet at Belbury, the headquarters of the NICE. First, in a parody of the biblical story of the tower of Babel ('that hyddeous strength', as an old Scots poem has it), Merlin produces pandemonium through a crazy confusion of language; then he causes carnage by releasing the animals kept at Belbury for the purpose of vivisection (a practice Lewis abhorred). At the end of the book Ransom returns to Perelandra to join Arthur and other heroes on the island of Aphallin (Avalon?); and Mark and Jane go to bed to enjoy connubial bliss.

If *Perelandra* had an element of incongruity, such as the occasional philosophizing on fish-back, the conjunction of the mundane and the supernatural in *That Hideous Strength* is incongruous in a way which borders too often on the grotesque, or even the plain silly. The whole Arthurian theme, while partly a tribute to Charles Williams (whose Arthurian poem *Taliessin through Logres* is mentioned in the book (cf. *CT* 550)), is also an attempt to introduce 'strangeness and beauty' into modern England. If this were to work, it would have to be done more subtly than it is in this book, where, it has to be said, Lewis is probably just trying to do too many things at once. It is in evoking other worlds, as he does in the first two books in the science-fiction trilogy, and later in *The Great Divorce*, and above all in *The Chronicles of Narnia*, that he is most successful.

4

Telling It (Almost) Straight: Apologies

Lewis's fame in the 1940s rested largely on his work as a Christian apologist – that is, a defender of the faith by means of rational argument. So little did Lewis seek this kind of fame that, when he was first approached by a publisher who had been impressed by *The Pilgrim's Regress* and *Out of the Silent Planet*, and wanted Lewis to contribute a book 'on pain' to the 'Christian Challenge' series, Lewis wished the book to appear anonymously. He did not get his way, although, when *The Problem of Pain* was published in 1940, it did contain a preface in which Lewis disclaimed any particular suitability to write as a Christian theologian on the subject of pain. The only purpose of the book is, Lewis says (perhaps none too modestly), 'to solve the intellectual problem raised by suffering' (*PP*, p. vii). This so-called problem of evil, a central issue in any defence of Christian belief, is addressed in 'theodicy' – that is, the attempt to vindicate the justice (Greek *dikē*) of God. The case against God is very clear and long established. Lewis sums it up thus: '"If God were good, He would wish to make His creatures perfectly happy, and if God were almighty He would be able to do that if He wished. But the creatures are not happy. Therefore God lacks either goodness, or power, or both." This is the problem of pain, in its simplest form' (*PP* 14). If Lewis's formulation recalls countless examination questions from introductory Philosophy of Religion courses, it also gives one reason why Lewis himself was for many years an atheist. He begins his book with the case against God of Lewis the atheist; the indictment is in essence the same as the classical formulation given above, but is expressed with a rhetorical panache typical of Lewis:

> All stories will come to nothing: all life will turn out in the end to have been a transitory and senseless contortion upon the idiotic face of infinite matter. If you ask me to believe that this is the work of a benevolent and omnipotent spirit, I reply that all the evidence points in the opposite direction. Either there is no spirit behind the universe, or else a spirit indifferent to good and evil, or else an evil spirit. (*PP* 2–3)

The first move of Lewis the apologist against Lewis the atheist is to question whether the origin of religious belief ever *did* depend on the evidence of 'the facts'. As he puts it: 'The spectacle of the universe as revealed by experience can never have been the ground of religion: it must always have been something in spite of which religion, acquired from a different source, was held' (*PP* 3). Thus theodicy is subsequent to, and never the source of, religious belief (cf. *PP* 4). Christianity is not the conclusion of a philosophical argument, but 'an awkward fact' which 'creates, rather than solves, the problem of pain' (*PP* 12). There are four basic elements of Christian belief, Lewis says. For the first element Lewis uses Rudolf Otto's term 'the experience of the *Numinous*' or religious awe (*PP* 4–5). This is the closest Lewis gets in this book to a purely experiential basis for religious belief, and it is interesting that he refers to experiences of 'awe' rather than those of 'Joy' which were crucial to his own conversion. However, the experiences Lewis narrates in *Surprised by Joy* do contain an element of numinous awe as well as of 'Sweet Desire'; and the experiences that Otto describes in *The Idea of the Holy* reveal the deep attractiveness as well as the awesomeness of 'the Holy', as his phrase 'the *mysterium tremendum et fascinans*' indicates. The examples Lewis gives of the Numinous come, predictably enough, from Wordsworth, Malory, Ovid, Aeschylus, and *The Wind in the Willows* (the latter example being the encounter of Rat and Mole with Pan). Lewis wants to distinguish sharply between, on the one hand, fear of specific dangers; and, on the other, dread of the Numinous or the Uncanny (*PP* 5). There is a gap, both in experience and in logic, between fear of danger, and awe of the Numinous, Lewis says; the latter could never be inferred from the former (*PP* 7). The transition from fear to awe is a 'sheer jump', analogous to the jump from empirical descriptions to aesthetic (and also moral) judgements (*PP* 8); it is either due to 'a mere twist in the human mind', or it is 'a direct experience of the really supernatural, to which the name Revelation might properly be given' (*PP* 8–9). Although Lewis is quite willing to refer to Freud on other occasions (and indeed alludes to him on the following page), he makes no reference here to the relevance of Freud's exploration of 'the Uncanny' to this 'mere twist in the human mind'. This might be due to ignorance on Lewis's part, but it is more likely that he is not interested in anything which would complicate the absolute dichotomy he is setting up between two explanations, one of which is presented as patently absurd, leaving the supernaturalist explanation as the only alternative.

This use of the rather crude argumentative device of the *reductio ad absurdum* (which may well derive from his father's work as a prosecuting solicitor in the Belfast police courts) is typical of Lewis the argufier. It recurs in his cursory treatment of the second element of religious belief, moral experience, when the reader is forced to view such experience as '*either* inexplicable illusion, *or else* revelation' (*PP* 10, emphasis added). The third element of religious belief – that is, the identification of the source of moral experience with the object of numinous awe – receives an equally terse and reductive treatment: it is either 'madness' or 'a revelation' (*PP* 11). The fourth and final element of Christian belief is the identification of the source of moral experience and the object of numinous awe with Jesus of Nazareth. This is Lewis's most famous *reductio ad absurdum*, to which he often returned. Either Jesus is 'a raving lunatic of an unusually abominable type, or else He was, and is, precisely what He said. There is no middle way' (*PP* 12). It was in a radio talk, broadcast in 1942 and subsequently published in *Mere Christianity*, that Lewis gave his most outrageous version of this 'shocking alternative'. Unless Jesus really is God, his claim to forgive sins is 'so preposterous as to be comic' (*MC* 52). If Jesus is not God, then:

> he would either be a lunatic – on a level with the man who says he is a poached egg – or else he would be the Devil of Hell. You must make your choice. Either this man was, and is, the Son of God: or else a madman or something worse. You can shut Him up for a fool, you can spit at Him and kill him as a demon; or you can fall at His feet and call Him Lord and God. (*MC* 52–3)

To suggest that Jesus was merely a great moral teacher is, Lewis says, 'patronising nonsense' (*MC* 53), a phrase which, in the heat of his rhetoric, Lewis may have failed to notice is a double-edged sword. If Lewis had really wanted to follow in the footsteps of Kierkegaard and the early Karl Barth, and be calculatedly offensive in his proclamation of the 'Absolute Paradox' of the Gospel, then why is he in this book and elsewhere presenting quite traditional arguments for the existence of God based on 'the Law of Human Nature'? Explanation and defence of 'mere Christianity' to unbelieving neighbours (*MC* 6) is the traditional vocation of the Christian apologist, for which Lewis, with his commitment to the role of reason in Christian belief, was suitably qualified. But the rhetoric of 'the scandal of particularity' (that is, the insistence that a Christian must believe at least one impossible thing – the Divinity of Jesus of Nazareth – before breakfast) does not sit comfortably with the kind of natural theology to which Lewis inclined. It is not clear whether Lewis's lapses into an alien register at crucial points in his theological arguments are due to his self-confessed amateur status as theologian (*PP*, p. viii); or to an inherited propensity to bludgeon interlocutors; or to the fact that his reasoned approach to belief was liable to give way under pressure. Perhaps all of the above. At any rate, it is unsettling to be told at the conclusion of the first chapter of *The Problem of Pain*: 'If any message from the core of reality were ever to reach us, we should expect to find in it just that unexpectedness, that wilful, dramatic anfractuosity which we find in the Christian faith. It has the master touch – the rough, male taste of reality, not made by us, or indeed, for us, but hitting us in the face' (*PP* 13). To formulate his or (*a fortiori*) *her* response to such language, the reader might well turn more profitably to psychoanalysis than to philosophy.

But if on such grounds, or better ones (as Lewis adds with modesty, doubtless to the relief of some readers), we become Christians, then we are saddled with the problem of pain (*PP* 13). Lewis's treatment of this problem is interesting from several points of view, though it is not original in its central philosophical or theological content. But the clarity and vividness of Lewis's style bring alive issues which most of his readers (not professional theologians) would not have considered before; or as Austin Farrer aptly puts it: '[Lewis] gives to textbook matter the freshness of a living reconsideration.'[1] Lewis's approach is to qualify the terms of the syllogism in which the problem of evil (or pain) is classically expressed. When we say that God is omnipotent or all-powerful, what do we mean? God cannot perform what is logically impossible, says Lewis; or, as he puts it: 'meaningless combinations of words do not suddenly acquire meaning simply because we prefix to them the two other words "God can"' (*PP* 16). And for God to make the kind of souls he desires, a stable, external environment is required. Such an external framework has to have fixed laws, even if (or perhaps: so that) God can very occasionally modify them in what we call miracles (*PP* 22). But only very occasionally, for to override the laws of nature too regularly would defeat the moral purpose of making souls which are freely loving and obedient.

Although the discussion of miracles and the laws of nature points forward to Lewis's later book *Miracles*, it is only the chapter on Divine Omnipotence in which it occurs that could properly be called philosophical. As Austin Farrer suggests, the rest of *The Problem of Pain* is theological.[2] Having established the necessary constraints of a rule-governed environment, Lewis goes on to discuss God's goodness; that is, how, within the context of that environment, God works to bring the creatures he has made to the happiness he desires for them, through their freely chosen love and obedience. In fact the ensuing argument is less theological than moral. Lewis's theology as well as his philosophy is so dominated by his moral idealism that, says Farrer, what is a strength 'runs into excess and overbalances it', so that 'Lewis risks forfeiting the sympathy of a compassionate reader'.[3] But excessive moralism alone would not have led Lewis to the highly speculative and at times eccentric (if not actually unorthodox) suggestions in the second part of the book. As Farrer puts it:

> Moralism of itself would not have carried him as far as this. Imagination has slipped from the leash of reason – even if it is a traditionalist imagination. His readers rub their eyes, and wonder what they are seeing – Lewis wrote fairy tales but surely he did not believe them! It adds to our stupefaction, rather than detracting from it, when he solemnly submits such fantasies to the censure of the Church.[4]

What Farrer refers to as 'fantasies' include elaborate accounts of the pre-lapsarian existence, and subsequent Fall, not only of humanity, but also of animals. However dubious these fantasies may be to orthodox theologians, they are of considerable interest to those interested in Lewis's imaginative writing. The description of what Lewis calls 'Paradisal man' strikingly anticipates the accounts of the King and Queen of Perelandra. Similarly, the account of Hell anticipates *The Great Divorce,* as when Lewis writes: 'the doors of hell are locked on the *inside.* I do not mean that the ghosts may not *wish* to come out of hell, in the vague fashion wherein an envious man "wishes" to be happy: but they certainly do not will even the first preliminary stages of that self-abandonment through which alone the soul can reach any good' (*PP* 115, emphasis in original). And whatever the absurdities and the anthropocentric bias of Lewis's chapter on 'Animal Pain', he does at least show a genuine interest in the experience of animals – and Aslan makes a very early appearance at the end of this chapter.

If Lewis's imagination has (whether to the amusement or the disapproval of the reader) 'slipped from the leash of reason' in *The Problem of Pain,* then reason is firmly in control in the radio addresses collected as *Mere Christianity* (1952). Or, to use the terms of Lewis's essay 'Bluspels and Flalansferes', there is in *The Problem of Pain* the occasional flash of a 'Pupil's metaphor', where Lewis would be hard pressed to put into plainer language his speculations on heaven, or on pre-lapsarian consciousness, whether animal or human. By contrast, *Mere Christianity* is very much more dominated by the 'Master's metaphor', where Lewis uses a variety of clever metaphors and analogies to sugar the pill of orthodox Christian doctrine. There is no doubt that in *Mere Christianity* metaphor is most often a means of expression rather than a mode of thought, to use the terms of *The Allegory of Love.* Faith is based on reason, Lewis says (*MC* 120); it is 'the act of holding on to things that your reason has once accepted, in spite of your changing moods' (*MC* 121). The enemy of faith is not reason, but imagination and emotions (*MC* 120). The latter are reduced to mere 'moods', which need to be taught 'where they get off' (*MC* 121). No doubt Lewis's approach and register in *Mere Christianity* have much to do with the audience he was addressing. Perhaps he felt that 'the dialectic of desire' was not quite appropriate for the BBC in the 1940s! But what emerges in *Mere Christianity* is a breezy confidence, and even a kind of slickness, in his use of rational argument.

Concurrent with Lewis's growing reputation as a radio broadcaster was his starring role in Oxford's best-attended debating society in the 1940s, the Socratic Club, founded in December 1941, to discuss 'the *pros* and *cons* of the Christian religion'. Lewis was the Club's President, as well as its hero. To the delight of his followers, many of them young women, the 'bonny fighter'[5] would regularly demolish his – preferably atheist – opponents with a relish and a vigour that would have made his father, the Belfast prosecuting solicitor, proud. The halcyon days lasted until February 1948 when Lewis met his nemesis in the formidable shape of Elizabeth Anscombe, a pupil of Wittgenstein, and later Professor of Philosophy at Cambridge. Anscombe, who, far from being an atheist, was a devout Roman Catholic and an admirer of St Thomas Aquinas, offered a robust critique of chapter III of Lewis's recently published book *Miracles* (1947). This chapter was entitled 'The Self-Contradiction of the Naturalist', and is only available in the original 1947 edition, since as a result of Anscombe's criticisms the chapter was substantially rewritten for the 1960 Fontana edition. Chapter III of *Miracles* is pivotal to Lewis's overall argument, which seeks to demonstrate the rationality of a supernaturalist interpretation of reality, so that the general *possibility* of miracles is established (Lewis eschews any detailed discussion of particular historical events claimed to be miraculous). By 'supernaturalist' Lewis does not in the first instance mean anything more dramatic than the view which resists the 'naturalist' claim that 'every finite thing or event must be (in principle) explicable in terms of the Total System' (*M.* 23; *M.*^{2} 29). 'Supernaturalism' does not even necessarily claim that miracles do in fact occur, only that they are possible. It does claim that we cannot say that the universe is rationally intelligible (the presupposition of science) unless there is some principle or reality beyond 'nature' – that is, beyond the 'Total System' explicable (in principle) by science. The very project of a total explanation depends on the principle guiding that explanation *not* being included in the total explanation. Or, as Derrida puts it in his famous diagnosis of 'the metaphysics of presence', the structure of Western thinking demands a 'centre', but that centre 'does not belong to the totality (is not part of the totality), [rather] the totality *has its centre elsewhere*' (emphasis in original).[6] But far from wishing to 'decentre' classical thought or deconstruct the idea of 'truth', Lewis in his philosophical writing wants to defend 'Truth' (with a capital T), and a metaphysics with knobs on.

This is where chapter III of *Miracles* comes in. Here Lewis asserts that: 'Unless human reasoning is valid no science can be true' (*M.* 26; *M.*[2]18); he is unwilling to entertain the notion that the sceptical or pragmatist diffidence about truth can possibly be in earnest. But if human reasoning itself is explained by the Total System out of which it evolves, it ceases in Lewis's view to be the valid human reasoning on which the scientific explanation depends in the first place. Hence 'naturalism' is self-refuting – and 'supernaturalism' wins the day. Despite the fact that *Miracles* is a much more seriously intended work than the broadcast talks with their knock-down arguments, there is still an element of the *reductio ad absurdum* argument which Lewis always wielded with such relish. As Anscombe, trained in the discipline of fine philosophical analysis, pointed out, Lewis's weapon was getting pretty blunt. The terms of his argument, such as 'causation' and 'validity', needed considerable clarification. Lewis's philosophical bombast simply did not stand up to close scrutiny.

There are differing accounts of this famous encounter. One version sees Lewis as devastated and humiliated; 'he had lost everything and was come to the foot of the Cross', as Hugo Dyson put it.[7] Anscombe herself appears to think that the reports of Lewis's philosophical demise were greatly exaggerated, and that the accounts of the debate by some of Lewis's friends, who seemed uninterested in (or who perhaps did not follow) the actual arguments, were 'an interesting example of the phenomenon called "projection"'.[8] As Anscombe says in the same place, Lewis did rewrite the chapter to take account of her criticisms, and the revised version is in her view a considerable improvement, even if it still 'has much to criticize in it'. Perhaps the most balanced view is the one that holds that Lewis had simply underestimated the extent to which the ground rules of professional philosophy had changed since he himself had trained as a philosopher. As his pupil George Sayer puts it: 'Jack could not cope with such developments [in philosophy] and really had no desire to. They made what he regarded as philosophical thinking almost impossible. "I can never write another book of that sort," he said to me of *Miracles*. And he never did.'[9]

What Lewis did write was *The Chronicles of Narnia*, and it is to these that we shall turn in the next chapter. Meanwhile we should look briefly at two works from the 1940s which straddle the divide between the 'straight' apologetic writing we have been discussing, and the mythopoeic approach of the science-fiction works. These 'mixed-genre' texts are *The Screwtape Letters* (1942) and *The Great Divorce* (1946). The former is probably the most famous and commercially successful of Lewis's works apart from *The Chronicles of Narnia*. Although *The Screwtape Letters* is sometimes classified by critics as one of Lewis's apologetic works, Lewis himself listed it in a letter as one of the works in which he said he was led 'to embody my religious belief in symbolical or mythopoeic forms, ranging from *Screwtape* to a kind of theologized science-fiction' (*L.* 444). Clearly *The Screwtape Letters* is at the opposite end of the range from *Out of the Silent Planet*. It is essentially a witty and at times penetrating tract on moral theology, set in the imaginative framework of a correspondence between a trainee devil, Wormwood, and his mentor, Screwtape. The book hardly works on the level of myth, however. There is, for example, no evocation of the kind of symbolic landscape which figures so prominently in Lewis's properly mythopoeic writings. Within its ingenious framework, *The Screwtape Letters* seeks to guide the reader to moral insight by means of critical reflection. Indeed, in a nice piece of irony, Screwtape advises Wormwood in his first letter to keep 'his patient' away from argument because 'the trouble with argument is that it moves the whole struggle onto the Enemy's own ground. . . . By the very act of arguing, you awake the patient's reason; and once it is awake, who can foresee the result?' (*SL* 12).

The Great Divorce: A Dream divides critics on the issue of how much it appeals to the head (and is part of the canon of Lewis's apologetic works), and how much to the heart, offering itself as myth to the reader's imaginative embrace. Respected Lewis critics weigh in on either side; perhaps Owen Barfield gets closest to the truth when he writes: '*The Great Divorce*. . . is a kind of myth and in that book, as perhaps not quite in any other, this ever diverse pair – . . . rational Lewis and mythopoeic Lewis – I will not say unite, but they do at least join hands' .[10] Certainly the mythical element of *The Great Divorce*, which Lewis refers to in the Preface as 'an imaginative supposal' (*GD* 9), is fragmented and dispersed among the various acutely observed vignettes of moral and spiritual failure, often reminiscent of *The Screwtape Letters*. But there are, though this may be a matter of individual 'taste', moments of genuine imaginative power. Lewis is at his mythopoeic best when describing symbolic landscapes, 'regions of strangeness and beauty', inhabited by mythological figures. In a different way from the science-fiction books, 'Lewis', the narrator of *The Great Divorce*, is 'out' of the silent planet we call Earth:

> The light and coolness that drenched me were like those of summer morning, early morning a minute or two before the sunrise, only that there was a certain difference. I had the sense of being in a larger space, perhaps even a larger *sort* of space, than I had ever known before: as if the sky were further off and the extent of the green plain wider than they could be on this little ball of earth. I had got 'out' in some sense which made the Solar System itself seem an indoor affair. (*GD* 26, emphasis in original)

The terrifyingly beautiful landscape of 'the Valley of the Shadow of Life' is realized with considerable power; indeed, because it is far more 'real' than the insubstantial ghosts who are on a day trip from Hell, it is to them, from the smallest blade of grass to the river itself, diamond hard. Lewis had got this general idea, as well as the particular idea of raindrops that would pierce the ghosts (including 'Lewis') like bullets, from an American pulp-science-fiction magazine (*GD* 9). But not only are the landscape, and the mythological figures such as the herd of unicorns (*GD* 58), realized much more fully than is the case, for example, in *The Pilgrim's Regress*; the character sketches too are at times devastatingly realistic. It is true that the balance of didacticism and fantasy in *The Great Divorce* is a delicate one. But for some of us it does work, and I would agree with A. N. Wilson that '*The Great Divorce* shows Lewis at his very best; it is something approaching a masterpiece'.[11]

5

The Christian Imaginary: Narnia

Towards the end of *Miracles*, that ambitious if flawed attempt to defend the Christian faith by rational argument, Lewis hints in a footnote at quite another way of presenting the truth he believed in. Dismissing reductionist views which see Myth as either 'misunderstood history', 'diabolical illusion', or 'priestly lying', Lewis says that Myth is, 'at its best, a real though unfocused gleam of divine truth falling on human imagination' (*M.* 161; *M.*^{2} 138). As we have already seen, for Lewis Myth offers a 'taste' of truth, and invites an 'imaginative embrace', rather than any merely cognitive assent. Sometimes what an author seeks to communicate is too subtle, too elusive, too *close*, to be caught in rational concepts. As Lewis puts it in his essay 'On Stories', sometimes only the net of narrative can get near to catching the bird, in this case, of paradise (cf. *OTOW* 45). The footnote in *Miracles* concludes in a vein which anticipates Lewis's later and more successful attempt to talk about miracles, and indeed 'the Grand Miracle' of the Incarnation itself, in the form of *stories*: 'The *story* of Christ demands from us, and repays, not only a religious and historical but also an *imaginative* response. It is directed to the child, the poet, and the savage in us as well as to the conscience and to the intellect. One of its functions is to break down dividing walls.' (*M.* 161; *M.*^{2} 138, emphasis added).

However traumatic the Anscombe affair of 1948 may, or may not, have been for Lewis, there is in the late 1940s and early 1950s a decisive shift away from apologetic writing, and an immersion in the quite different genre of the fairy tale. Indeed, there was much in Lewis's life during these years to drive him to seek the 'recovery, escape and consolation' which Tolkien said were characteristic of the fairy story.[1] Not the least of Lewis's worries in this period was, ironically, the cooling of his friendship with Tolkien.[2] Other 'stress factors' (to use a phrase which might have drawn comment from Lewis) were: the increasing senility of 'Minto' (Mrs Moore) and the unknown expense of keeping her in residential care until her death (in fact she died in 1951); the painfully regular alcoholic 'benders' of his brother; a very heavy workload; and a sense of malaise and deprivation in what seemed to Lewis a bleak post-war Britain. In these circumstances, the backless wardrobe (derived probably from E. Nesbit and George MacDonald) must have seemed like an escape hatch. Whether we interpret such a resort to fairy-tale images in the face of stress as a form of 'escapism', or as a sane and healthy response to a situation which had led in 1949 to Lewis's physical collapse, in fact it seems as if Lewis had little conscious control over the images; he says that they just came to him.

In the various accounts which Lewis subsequently gave of his writing of the Narnia books, he emphasizes his passive role in the process. 'Making' a story is not the best way to describe a process which for Lewis was more like bird-watching (*OTOW* 68). He continues: 'I see pictures. Some of these pictures have a common flavour, almost a common smell, which groups them together. Keep quiet and watch and they will begin joining themselves up' (*OTOW* 68). In Lewis's experience these pictures never joined themselves up so consistently as to form a complete story. There were always for him 'gaps' which needed to be filled up by 'some deliberate inventing' (*OTOW* 68). But, he insists, 'the images always came first'. In the case of *The Lion, the Witch and the Wardrobe* the images or 'mental pictures' which 'bubbled up' were 'a faun carrying an umbrella, a queen on a sledge, [and] a magnificent lion'. 'At first,' he adds, 'there wasn't even anything Christian about them' (*OTOW* 73). As these images sorted themselves into events (i.e. became a story), they demanded a Form, and the Form which presented itself, and with which Lewis says he 'fell in love', was that of the Fairy Tale (*OTOW* 73). For Lewis a great advantage of the fairy tale genre is that it circumvents the overly reverential attitude of conventional religious belief, which, he says, can 'freeze feelings' and, with its lowered voices, make the whole business of religion seem 'almost something medical' (*OTOW* 73). The fairy-tale form has an 'inflexible hostility to all analysis, digression, reflections and "gas"' (*OTOW* 73). The latter features are doubtless intended by Lewis to be seen as elements of the realist novel, but they might also perhaps be seen as characteristic of his own apologetic writing. But by casting his religious beliefs into an imaginary world, where vivid pictures are caught in the net of a fantastic narrative, might not some of these beliefs 'appear in their real potency?', Lewis asks. 'Could one,' he continues (and one wonders to what extent Elizabeth Anscombe is still at the back of his mind), 'steal past those watchful dragons?' (*OTOW* 73).

But is there also in the passage just quoted, with its references to 'paralysing inhibitions' and 'frozen feelings', to 'lowered voices' in relation to 'something medical', an echo of a much earlier trauma than the one Lewis may have experienced at the hands of Elizabeth Anscombe? Does the apparent loss of confidence in a familiar, stable world, which revolved around clever Jack the intellectual Giant-Killer, resonate with the much earlier loss of 'all settled happiness, all that was tranquil and reliable' (*SBJ* 23), when his mother died? The fairy tale might not only allow Lewis to steal past an overly intellectualized and conventional kind of religion; it might also allow Jack to steal back to 'the old security' of his original relationship with his mother, of which the later 'stabs of Joy' are arguably the echoes. The essays on fairy tales are full of the language of love and longing. As one of them says of a boy reading: 'fairy land arouses a longing for he knows not what. It stirs and troubles him ... with the dim sense of something beyond his reach.... the boy reading the fairy-tale desires and is happy in the very fact of desiring' (*OTOW* 65). The Narnian fairy tales embody 'the imaginary' not only in the conventional sense, but also in the psychoanalytical sense of the realm where the beginnings of the child's being and doing are played out in relation to its mother. *The Chronicles of Narnia* are overdetermined in that they are *both* religiously motivated 'allegories of love' à la Spenser (they are Lewis's 'miniature *Faerie Queene*'), *and* unconsciously motivated 'tales of love' à la Kristeva, where the self seeks the healing of a primal wound through the invocation and the evocation of the 'primary maternal matrix'.

THE LION, THE WITCH AND THE WARDROBE

There is some debate over the order in which *The Chronicles of Narnia* should be read. Some critics, and on one occasion Lewis himself,[3] have recommended the chronological order – that is, starting with *The Magician's Nephew* which recounts the beginnings of 'all the comings and goings between our own world and the land of Narnia', and indeed the beginnings of Narnia itself. However, the consensus now seems to be that it is better to read the Chronicles in the order of publication, not least because much of the impact of a first reading of *The Lion, the Witch and the Wardrobe* is lost if the reader is already familiar with Narnia. The question which dominates the early chapters of *The Lion, the Witch and the Wardrobe* is the very existence of Narnia. Lucy's first stumbling into Narnia through the wardrobe is a moment of real magic, equal to anything in George MacDonald or Lewis Carroll. But, like the existence of the Princess's magical great-great-grandmother in MacDonald's *The Princess and the Goblin*, the existence of Narnia itself is a matter of faith. Lucy becomes distressed as not only the villainous Edmund and the slightly silly Susan, but even the stalwart Peter, will not take her discovery seriously. Peter and Susan, concerned about Lucy's mental health, seek the advice of the mysterious professor, who, unknown both to the children and to the readers (unless they have previously read *The Magician's Nephew*), had as a boy been in the first party of humans to visit Narnia. The professor makes no allusion to his own acquaintance with Narnia, but, in what one hopes is a piece of self-parody on Lewis's part, insists on the reign of logic in questions of belief in the supernatural. Echoing the famous knock-down argument in *Mere Christianity* that Jesus was bad, mad, or God, the professor declares that: 'Either your sister is telling lies, or is mad, or she is telling the truth' (*LWW* 47). Experience renders the first two unlikely, so logic demands belief in Narnia, on the basis of the available evidence; '... what *do* they teach them at these schools?', the professor wonders (*LWW* 49). Eventually in chapter six all the children do find their way into Narnia through the wardrobe, not through their own seeking, but because 'some magic in the house ... was chasing them into Narnia' (*LWW* 52). Like Joy, of which it is the embodiment, Narnia is never under our control; even when it is actively sought by calling upon Aslan, as in the beginning of *The Silver Chair*, that seeking is in reality a response to the prior calling of Aslan to the children (*SC* 25).

Tolkien was critical of *The Chronicles of Narnia*, in part because they did not conform very closely to his criteria for 'sub-creation' (and also perhaps because the Chronicles were initially far more successful than *The Lord of the Rings*!). Nevertheless the Narnia stories do exhibit some of the main features of Tolkien's account of the fairy story. Above all, they express the 'joy' which is for Tolkien 'the mark of the true fairy-story'.[4] Such joy is experienced in a 'fleeting glimpse . . . beyond the walls of the world, poignant as grief'.[5] It is particularly associated with the tale's sudden 'turn' towards the Happy Ending or *Eucatastrophe* (a word Tolkien coined): 'In such stories when the sudden 'turn' comes we get a piercing glimpse of joy, and heart's desire, that for a moment passes outside the frame . . . and lets a gleam come through'.[6] A dramatic example of such a joyous 'turn' comes in *The Lion, the Witch and the Wardrobe* when the Stone Table on which Aslan had been sacrificed cracks loudly, and the resurrected Aslan is suddenly standing behind Lucy and Susan, speaking to them. Tolkien calls such a glimpse of joy *evangelium* (good news or 'gospel') and explicitly links it with what for him is the greatest fairy tale of all: 'The Gospels contain a fairy-story, or a story of a larger kind which embraces all the essence of fairy-stories'.[7] For Tolkien there is an *analogy* between the Gospel story (authored by God[8]) and the fairy story; between Creation (God's story) and sub-creation (a human story). But in Lewis's fairy stories (and this may partly explain Tolkien's unease with them) the *difference* essential to the analogical identity-in-difference between 'the Christian story' and the fairy story seems in danger of being obliterated. As has already been suggested, Lewis the sub-creator appears to have some problems with the 'sub'. The death and resurrection of Aslan have a more powerful impact than any mere *analogy* to the death and resurrection of Christ; they do not merely 'partake of reality'[9] so much as they *are* in some sense that reality.

If such observations raise theological questions about Lewis's work, there are also some psychological questions to be asked. After encountering the risen Aslan, Lucy has a momentary panic as she wonders whether Aslan might be ghost. To reassure her, 'Aslan stooped his golden head and licked her forehead. The warmth of his breath and a rich sort of smell that seemed to hang about his hair came all over her' (*LWW* 147). One does not have to swallow everything in David Holbrook's *The Skeleton in the Wardrobe* to feel that he is right to see in the children's experience with the resurrected Aslan the suggestion of a fantasy reconciliation between Lewis and his mother who died. Even if Lewis had not, as we shall see, spilled the beans in *The Magician's Nephew*, it would have been tempting to read *The Chronicles of Narnia*, not only as a quest for Joy, but also as a quest for his lost mother. For Holbrook (who partly bases his thesis on Lewis's intense reaction to MacDonald's quest for *his* lost mother in *Phantastes*), the trauma of Lewis's bereavement when he was 9 years old reactivated an older and deeper sense of loss or lack somewhere in Lewis's earliest experience. Grounding his interpretation on Winnicott's view that play with the mother has a crucial role in fostering in the very young infant the beginnings of a sense of 'being' and 'reality', Holbrook postulates some kind of failure in Lewis's earliest environment. Unlike the case of George MacDonald where, remarkably, there actually is evidence of a traumatic weaning,[10] there is in Lewis's case limited relevant biographical material, and Holbrook has to base his diagnosis largely on an ingenious reading of Lewis's fairy tales. Whatever we may make of some of Holbrook's more rebarbative translations of Lewis's fairy stories into psycho-analytical jargon, it is nevertheless hard to dismiss his claim that something to do with the creative power of play in the 'primary maternal matrix' is at work in, for example, the following description of a post-resurrection romp with Aslan:

> Laughing, though she didn't know why, Lucy scrambled over to reach him. Aslan leaped again. A mad chase began. Round and round the hill-top he led them, now hopelessly out of their reach, now letting them almost catch his tail, now diving between them, now tossing them in the air with his huge and beautifully velveted paws and catching them again, and now stopping unexpectedly so that all three of them rolled over together in a happy laughing heap of fur and arms and legs. (*LWW* 148–9)

To the obvious question of how such a *male* figure as Aslan can be associated with the mother, one answer might be that in the earliest pre-oedipal scenario 'objects' (that is, 'persons') have not yet been fully constituted, let alone gendered. For the very young infant, the mother is an 'environment' rather than a person – thus Lucy cannot decide whether the romp is 'more like playing with a thunderstorm or playing with a kitten' (*LWW* 149). Another, more controversial, response would be to invoke Julia Kristeva's notion of 'the imaginary father'. In Freudian and post-Freudian psychoanalysis the figure of the Father dominates in the Oedipal situation, which is a more or less unhappily resolved struggle between the desires of three persons: the Father, the Mother, and the child. The Oedipal Father also figures as the Lacanian Phallus, dominating the so-called Symbolic Order; and as the Judaeo-Christian God, dominating his creation. Somewhat controversially, Kristeva has proposed a positive role for the desire of the father in the *pre*-oedipal realm, which had tended to be seen as an exclusively maternal domain. Her 'imaginary father' is not yet at this stage the Father as a full person or 'object'; it is an 'otherness' in the otherwise damagingly exclusive interpenetration of desire in the 'primary maternal matrix'. The 'imaginary father' may pre-figure the Oedipal Father, but 'he' plays a more nurturing and creative role in the early development of the child. Aslan seems to oscillate between, on the one hand, a playful and intimately tactile figure who evokes Kristeva's notion of 'the semiotic' – at his very name 'each one of the children felt something jump in its inside' (*LWW* 65); and, on the other, a terrifying and potentially punitive figure who, immediately after the romp just described, tells the girls to stop their ears because he intends to roar: 'And Aslan stood up and when he opened his mouth his face became so terrible that they did not dare to look at it. And they saw all the trees in front of him bend before the blast of his roaring as grass bends in a meadow before the wind' (*LWW* 149). Holbrook in my view exaggerates what he calls the minatory or threatening aspect of Aslan, which he derives from the bullying and insane headmaster of 'Belsen', as Lewis's prep-school is called in *Surprised by Joy*. But, as we shall see below, the Chronicles do undeniably contain some disturbingly cruel scenes with Aslan.

Of the threatening quality of the White Witch, however, there can be no doubt. For Holbrook the Witch is the lost mother whose death is to the child the ultimate gesture of abandonment and rejection. Certainly the motif of the land frozen in perpetual winter, where it is 'always winter and never Christmas', is a powerful symbol for the emotional death wrought by the rejecting and possibly hostile aspect of the dead mother. But it is only an *aspect* of the lost mother. The mother does not yet exist as a whole person for the very young child, according to the 'object-relations theory' of Winnicott and Melanie Klein; 'she' is split into 'part objects', which may, or may not, be integrated into a 'whole object' to which the child, by growing into a 'whole object' (i.e. by becoming a self), can begin to relate. The suggestion is that for Lewis the trauma of his mother's death exacerbated some already existing failure properly to integrate the 'parts' of 'himself' and his mother into viable selves. In technical terms, Lewis remained stuck in Klein's 'paranoid-schizoid' position, with the Witch representing the terrifyingly cruel and rejecting Bad Mother (or 'Breast'), and Aslan representing (for at least some of the time) the ultimately satisfying and desirable Good Mother (or 'Breast'). Kristeva seems to be saying something quite similar to Klein and Winnicott, though in different terms, when she talks of the 'abjection' of the mother. The 'abject' is the abjected mother; it is terrifying, uncanny, and repulsive, precisely because it transgresses any defining limits which might stabilize and secure a human identity. It is paradigmatically the 'undead', or the vampire; one of the clearest examples in literature of the 'abject' is George MacDonald's *Lilith*.[11] Significantly the White Witch is not human, though she appears to be; as Mr Beaver tells the children, she is a daughter of Lilith, not of Eve (*LWW* 76). Mr Beaver continues in a passage which is genuinely disturbing: 'But there's no two views about things that look like humans and aren't. . . . take my advice, and when you meet anything that's going to be human and isn't yet, or used to be human once and isn't now, or ought to be human and isn't, you keep your eyes on it and feel for your hatchet' (*LWW* 77). Terrifying as the Witch may be, it is even more terrifying to find an exemplar of 'live-and-let-live' decency exhibiting such ferocious paranoia. This is the violence which is truly unsettling in Lewis's work, and not the mildly realistic battle scenes to which Holbrook rather moralistically objects.

Lewis's first Narnian fairy tale does, of course, have a Happy

Ending. The wicked Witch is killed by the resurrected Aslan, the children are made Kings and Queens of Narnia, and 'long and happy was their reign'. At first much of their time is spent in 'seeking out the remnants of the White Witch's army and destroying them . . . But in the end all that evil brood was stamped out' (*LWW* 166). And once the threateningly 'other', or the 'abject', has been eliminated, the children can get on with promoting Lewis's version of 'the good life', with its embryonic concerns for ecology and animal rights: 'And they made good laws and kept the peace and saved good trees from being unnecessarily cut down, and liberated young dwarfs and young satyrs from being sent to school, and generally stopped busybodies and interferers and encouraged ordinary people who wanted to live and let live' (*LWW* 166). Such a vision is hardly utopian. But Lewis's message is not really to do with social justice or good citizenship or even with achieving personal integration. At bottom it is about the communication of Joy or, to use the term Lewis used in connection with *Phantastes*, a distinctive kind of 'Holiness' (even if, as in *Phantastes*, that 'Holiness' is constantly threatened by a 'dark side', emanating in some way from the dead mother[12]). Readers of *The Lion, the Witch and the Wardrobe* may each have their own moment when they get 'a piercing glimpse of joy'. It might be Lucy's first discovery of the snowy wood through the magic wardrobe; or the moment when the changing appearance of the wood forces the Witch's dwarf to exclaim: 'This is no thaw... This is *Spring*' (*LWW* 112); or the girls' exhilarating ride on Aslan from the Stone Table to the Witch's castle (*LWW* 149–50); or the moment when the children finally reach Cair Paravel, the castle where they are to be crowned and from which they are to rule Narnia:

> The castle at Cair Paravel on its little hill towered up above them; before them were the sands, with rocks and little pools of salt water, and seaweed, and the smell of the sea and long miles of bluish-green waves breaking for ever and ever on the beach. And oh, the cry of the sea-gulls! Have you heard it? Can you remember? (*LWW* 164)

And at the ensuing banquet (in what might almost be seen as a riposte to T. S. Eliot's *Prufrock*, a poem which Lewis intensely disliked), the children do hear the mermaids singing *to them*:

'And that night there was a great feast in Cair Paravel, and revelry and dancing, and gold flashed and wine flowed, and answering to the music inside, but stranger, sweeter, and more piercing, came the music of the sea people' (*LWW* 165). There is at certain points in *The Lion, the Witch and the Wardrobe* a degree of lyricism which reminds us that at his core Lewis was, if a poet *manqué,* nevertheless a poet.

PRINCE CASPIAN

Readers acquainted with *Surprised by Joy* will notice that the main elements of Joy – that is, myth (whether Greek or 'Northern'), medieval romance, and a romantic delight in nature – all reappear in *The Lion, the Witch and the Wardrobe.* These elements are even more markedly present in Lewis's next fairy tale, *Prince Caspian.* The medieval element is strongly present in that it is a tale of 'knights in armour', with detailed attention not only to the armour, the weapons, and the fighting, but also to Caspian's medieval education and the stylized wording of Peter's challenge to Miraz. The sense of 'medievalness' is intensified because not only is Narnia in itself always already 'medieval'; there is also *within* the story a nostalgia for a lost medieval past. Over a thousand Narnian years have elapsed since the children's last visit, but only one of *our* years has passed, so that the children have the uncanny experience of discovering the ruins of their own castle! The children have become mythical figures in the Narnian world they return to, just as if, as Peter says, 'we were Crusaders or Anglo-Saxons or someone coming back to modern England' (*PC* 34) – or indeed as if they were Merlin coming back to Bracton in *That Hideous Strength.* It is noticeable, however, that there is no *cultural* change in Narnia. In its entire 2,555-year history the culture remains in a loose sense 'medieval' or pre-technological (apart from the lamp-post in Lantern Wood!). Under bad rulers such as Miraz and Shift the Ape bad things happen, mainly cruelty to animals and the felling of good trees. But the world of Narnia lives and dies without being exposed to the (for Lewis) horrors of modern civilization, which he pillories elsewhere.

Lewis does not simply oppose 'nature' to 'culture' (as in

Romanticisms 6 and 7 in the list of Romanticisms in the Preface to *The Pilgrim's Regress*). He privileges one culture (the medieval) over others, both in his theoretical writing (especially in *The Discarded Image*), and in his fictional works. Yet there is in *Prince Caspian* a strong 'nature-versus-culture' theme, which culminates in the 'liberation' of the river-god of the Great River of Narnia from 'his chains' – that is, the Bridge of Beruna (*PC* 169–70). One would hardly have thought that a bridge is the epitome of technocracy, but there is an anarchic wildness on the loose in *Prince Caspian* which is perhaps more authentically Lewis than the ultra-conservative tendencies of which he is accused. The power which destroys the bridge, and a couple of schools, is Bacchus, also called Bromius, Bassareus, and the Ram (*PC* 137) – Lewis does not give him his original name, Dionysos, perhaps because of the Nietzschean association. Although Aslan has to be seen to be in control in *Prince Caspian*, the presence of Bacchus or Dionysos is very powerful in the book. Even the refrain that 'in all stories Aslan comes from over the sea' is an echo of the motif in Greek literature that the Stranger God, Dionysos, comes from over the sea. And when he comes, he comes with a vengeance. The epidemic of mania and violence brought by the god, who is, paradoxically, also called the bringer of peace, is most powerfully expressed in Euripides' *Bacchae*. As was noted above, Euripides' play had a great effect on the young Lewis, when 'the orgiastic drum-beat' entered his imagination. In a sentence which is relevant to the targeting of schools in the Bacchanalian 'Romp' (*sic*) in *Prince Caspian*, Lewis says in *Surprised by Joy* that 'the orgiastic drum-beat . . . was perhaps unconsciously connected with my growing hatred of the public school orthodoxies and conventions, my desire to tear and break it all' (*SBJ* 93). Lewis's description of the 'chap who might do anything – absolutely anything', as Edmund puts it (*PC* 137), is quite close to Euripides' Dionysos; he is dressed only in a faun skin and his face is slightly effeminate, 'almost too pretty for a boy's, if it had not looked so extremely wild' (*PC* 136).

The conclusion of *Prince Caspian* takes us very close to the heart of Lewis. One of those about to be liberated 'looked out of the window and saw the divine revellers singing up the street and a stab of joy went through her heart' (*PC* 172). *Pace* Lewis the critic in *The Personal Heresy*, we do get closely in touch with

Lewis the writer in a scene which anticipates the miraculous healing of Digory's (that is, Lewis's) dying mother in *The Magician's Nephew,* though here the dying woman is simply called 'Auntie'. In a scene of considerable psychological resonance, Aslan has to stoop down and squeeze into, and finally burst open, the woman's tiny cottage in order to get to her. She is cured by Aslan, but at this point Bacchus makes a significant entry: '"Here you are, mother," said Bacchus, dipping a pitcher in the cottage well and handing it to her. But what was in it now was not water but the richest wine...' (*PC* 174). The term 'mother' can be used, of course, as a generic term for an old woman, and here it is perhaps only in that sense that Lewis is consciously using it. But this coincidence of fiction with fact is too great not to suggest some deeper motivation at work, albeit unconsciously. This suggestion becomes even more plausible when it transpires that the old woman is Caspian's old nurse, and we remember that, in that striking passage in *Surprised by Joy* where Lewis describes the impact on him of the 'Holiness' of George MacDonald's *Phantastes,* his mother and his nurse are conflated (*SBJ* 145). And it is interesting that it is *Bacchus* who turns the water into wine. In his discussion in *Miracles* of the water-into-wine miracle at Cana, Lewis refers to 'the false god Bacchus' (*M.* 163; M.^{2}, 140). There he is emphasizing that Christ is the 'end' – in the sense of the *abolition* – of Bacchus. Here in *Prince Caspian* he seems to be emphasizing that Aslan, 'the (not so) hidden Christ of Narnia', is the 'end' – in the sense of the *fulfilment* – of Bacchus. Thus Aslan and Bacchus appear at times almost as partners, as a kind of 'dynamic duo', to use a phrase which seems not inappropriate to the carnivalesque conclusion of *Prince Caspian.*

THE VOYAGE OF THE 'DAWN TREADER'

Never again was Greek mythology to dominate a Chronicle of Narnia to the extent that it does in *Prince Caspian.* The episodic plot of *The Voyage of the 'Dawn Treader',* with its loosely linked adventures at sea, is obviously based on the *Odyssey,* though possibly no more than on the medieval *Voyage of St Brendan.* It is closer in spirit to Spenser than the first two Narnia books, and is more 'allegorical' in the sense that it is transparently dealing with 'sanctification and the disciplines of the Christian life'.[13] The children arrive on the *Dawn Treader* via a magic picture in a Cambridge bedroom, and the sea east of Narnia (they never actually set foot on Narnian soil). This can be read as entry into the 'ship' (or 'ark') of faith through baptism. The voyagers, and none more than Eustace, the new recruit to the English friends of Narnia, are given a series of lessons in Christian virtue, and especially in Temperance. 'Temperance' is to be understood in the broad sense of 'moderation' (as in book II of *The Faerie Queene*), and not in the narrow sense of 'teetotalism'. The latter is indeed one of the failings of the odious Eustace Clarence Scrubb (who, as Lewis says in a wonderful opening line, almost deserved his name). Other faults in Eustace include being a vegetarian, a pacifist, a non-smoker, and wearing a special kind of underclothes. He also takes vitamin supplements and does not read 'the right books' (e.g. about dragons), preferring 'books of information... [with] pictures of grain elevators or fat foreign children doing exercises in model schools' (*VDT* 7).

Lewis obviously presumes that his readers will share his deep prejudice against 'progressive' education. One of Eustace's problems, it is implied, is that he has never been given a sound thrashing, since his school (*'of course'*, says Lewis) has no corporal punishment (*VDT* 31, emphasis added). While Lewis's criticisms of certain educational developments, for example in *The Abolition of Man*, may have some validity, here it seems that Eustace is being made a scapegoat for Lewis's very entrenched and at times hardly rational attitude to modern education. What is odd is that Lewis's experiences at his prep school were by his own account brutal and distressing. Lewis may well have been done some lasting inner harm by the insane and abusive clergyman who ran 'Belsen'; he certainly seems to have been left with ambivalent love–hate feelings about school in general and beating in particular. Beating plays a significant part in his erotic fantasies, as his letters to his friend Arthur Greeves reveal. And there is something quite disturbing about the cruelty involved in Eustace's 'cure' .

On one of the islands which the *Dawn Treader* visits, Eustace slinks off to avoid the work involved in repairing and replenishing the ship. He gets lost, and to his horror, and subsequent relief, stumbles across a dragon in the process of dying. Caught in a torrential downpour, he takes refuge in the dead dragon's lair and falls asleep. In an almost Kafkaesque scene which is uncanny and comic at the same time, Eustace wakes and gradually realizes that he has turned into a dragon: 'Sleeping on a dragon's hoard with greedy, dragonish thoughts in his heart, he had become a dragon himself' (*VDT* 73). While it is true that it had occurred to Eustace that this new world into which he had stumbled might be a kind of tax haven, and that he might manage to make off with some of the dragon's hoard south of the border to Calormen (*VDT* 70), it would hardly be fair to describe the gains he thus contemplates as ill-gotten. He seems guilty only of a certain opportunism, with thoughts no more greedy than those of Caspian at the discovery of the magic pool which turns everything to gold (*VDT* 100). While Eustace is no doubt a 'record stinker', the particular punishment of dragonization does not seem specially appropriate, and there is even a kind of macabre vindictiveness when Lewis makes the vegetarian Eustace – once dragonized – eat the carcass of the other dragon.

But if Eustace's punishment by dragonization seems harsh, there is a disturbing cruelty in the manner of his cure. Eustace is led by Aslan to a pool and told to 'undress'. At first Eustace misunderstands, but then realizes that he is expected to tear his own skin off, 'as if it were a banana' (*VDT* 85). Three times Eustace peels his skin off, but each time finds another dragon skin underneath. Then Aslan says: 'You will have to let me undress you.' So, Eustace says, 'I just lay flat down on my back and let him do it... The first tear he made was so deep that I thought it had gone right into my heart' (*VDT* 86). Finally, after much pain, Eustace is freed of his dragon skin: 'he peeled the beastly stuff right off... and there was I smooth and soft as a peeled switch... Then he caught hold of me – I didn't like that much for I was very tender underneath now that I'd no skin on – and threw me into the water' (*VDT* 86). While the above description can no doubt be given a respectable allegorical interpretation, it also contains some rather unsettling sado-masochistic connotations.

If Eustace's villainy mainly seems to consist in being 'politically correct' *avant la lettre*, the book's real hero, Reepicheep the Talking Mouse, appears as a comic version of Chaucer's 'verray parfit gentil knight'. Lewis resisted the attempt to make an animated film version of *The Lion, the Witch and the Wardrobe*, especially one 'in the Disney line'[14]; yet some readers may find that Reepicheep can be almost as unbearably 'cute' as anything from the Disney stable. Nevertheless Reepicheep is given the highest destiny in the book; it is he who is on a quest for Joy, which began in his cradle when a dryad sang to him:

> Where sky and water meet,
> Where the waves grow sweet,
> Doubt not, Reepicheep,
> To find all you seek,
> There in the utter East.
>
> (*VDT* 21)

Finally, after many adventures – including encounters with a scary but rather stupid sea-monster, two retired stars, and a terrifying black hole where *dreams* (not day dreams) come true – Reepicheep finds his heart's desiring in the utter East. 'Quivering with happiness', he goes over the wave at the very End of the World in his coracle, and enters, we are assured, into Aslan's country (*VDT* 185).

The book might well have ended with this moment of genuine climax. However, Lewis chose to have a final scene in which the children come literally to the End of the World, where they meet a Lamb who 'in its sweet milky voice' invites them (as in John 21: 9–12) to come and breakfast on fish cooked on a fire. Some readers may find this an unfortunate shift of tone from 'allegory' in a good sense (the diminutive Reepicheep's story has an almost mythic grandeur) to 'allegory' in the bad sense of the didactic intrusion of edifying material from The Other Story, clumsily assimilated. Once again, Lewis's proclivity to mix 'neat' elements of the Christian story in with his own story tends to weaken the power and authenticity of both. Lewis seems determined to err on the side of obviousness, despite his knowledge that the best stories are elusive, that their narrative nets never quite catch what the story is *really* about (*OTOW* 44–5) – or as Lucy puts it after her amazing experiences with the Magician's Book, when the loveliest story she has ever read fades irretrievably from her mind: 'ever since that day what Lucy means by a good story is a story which reminds her of the forgotten story in the Magician's Book' (*VDT* 122).

THE SILVER CHAIR

The 'cured' Eustace is the hero of *The Silver Chair*, along with another new friend of Narnia, Jill Pole. The unpleasant 'co-educational' school, which had made such a 'record stinker' of Eustace, figures significantly at the beginning and end of the tale, which begins on a dull autumn day with Jill crying behind the gym. The narrator denies that this is going to be 'a school story', but in a sense it is. The answer to the Professor's reiterated question 'What *do* they teach them in these schools?' is, of course, 'not enough Plato'; *The Silver Chair* seeks to remedy this deficiency. The influence of Plato's Cave allegory on *The Silver Chair*'s climax, the dialogue between the Queen of Underland and the children, Puddleglum, and Prince Rilian, has already been noted; but the book as a whole is about 'knowing'. The central chapter is called 'How they discovered something worth knowing', and the main talking animals in this Chronicle are, naturally, owls. One critic has described the main theme of *The Silver Chair* as 'epistemological release'.[15]

However, the real theme of *The Silver Chair* is not so much the *getting* as the *keeping* of knowledge. Unlike Plato's allegory, the story does not start underground, but, after the prologue in school, in Heaven. Hounded by the bullies of 'Experiment House', Jill and Eustace invoke Aslan in a manner Eustace had learned from Ramandu (one of the retired stars in *Voyage of the 'Dawn Treader'*, and subsequently Caspian's father-in-law). They are transported not to Narnia itself, however, but directly to Aslan's country – that is, Heaven. As in *The Great Divorce*, Heaven is located on top of an enormously high cliff, from which Jill foolishly causes Eustace to fall. However, Eustace is saved by Aslan's breath, which blows him to Narnia. Aslan then confronts Jill, and sets her and Eustace the task of seeking Prince Rilian, the lost son of Caspian. To guide them on this quest, Aslan gives them four signs, which he makes Jill learn by heart. Much of the plot of *The Silver Chair* centres round whether Jill (and subsequently Eustace and Puddleglum, a froglike creature called a Marshwiggle) *remember* the signs. Aslan drills these signs into Jill in an example of the kind of rote learning which presumably is woefully lacking in Experiment House. Jill is told to repeat the signs morning, noon, and night, because: 'Here on the mountain, the air is clear and your mind is clear; as soon as you drop down into Narnia, the air will thicken... [and] confuse your mind' (*SC* 27). Then Jill too is blown by Aslan down into Narnia.

The idea of falling from Heaven into the world with the task of remembering, despite appearances, the true and the real is, of course, quintessentially Platonic. But the biblical emphasis on revelation and obedience is also present, so that it is a *Christian* Platonism to which the reader is being introduced. As in the Renaissance Christian Platonism of Sidney and Spenser, it is more a matter of knowing the truth with the heart than of understanding the truth with the head, more a matter of 'will' than 'wit' (see *EL* 345). And it is *poetry* which touches the parts mere philosophy cannot reach, by setting forth captivating images of virtue. As Lewis puts it in *The Abolition of Man*, 'without the aid of trained emotions the intellect is powerless' (*AOM* 19). The Narnia books follow in the tradition of Spenser in embodying 'in moving images the common wisdom' (see *EL* 386). In contrast to I. A. Richards, Lewis *welcomes* 'stock responses' to literature; creating them is primarily what literature is for (see *PPL* 54 ff.). All the Narnia books can be seen as attempts to train the reader's emotions by means of captivating images, by letting 'the pictures tell you their own moral' (*OTOW* 69). But *The Silver Chair* is more explicitly *about* the role of the emotions in preserving the memory of the true and the real than any other of the Chronicles.

The Silver Chair is also the most literary of the Chronicles. Its atmosphere and at times its diction are reminiscent of Malory and Spenser. Prince Rilian is explicitly compared with Hamlet (*SC* 123). The witch, being of the same kind as the White Witch of *The Lion, the Witch and the Wardrobe*, is descended from Lilith, especially as she appears in George MacDonald's *Lilith;* she also seems related to Geraldine in Coleridge's 'Christabel'. The whole Underland sequence is strongly reminiscent of MacDonald's *The Princess and the Goblin*, and the Really Deep Land of Bism, a kind of underground Paradise, connects, via MacDonald, with the German Romantic fascination with mines and underground mysteries. But the most sustained and important intertext for *The Silver Chair* is *The Faerie Queene*. The 'silver chair' itself appears in the Cave of Mammon sequence, when Guyon is led to the Garden of Proserpina (goddess of the Underworld), in the midst of which stands 'a siluer seat' (*FQ* II. vii. 51–3). Guyon resists the temptation to take the golden fruit of the garden and to sit on the 'siluer stoole' which is 'the chair of forgetfulness' (*FQ* II. vii. 63). And, as Cox has pointed out, the struggle of Rilian with the Green Witch, who transforms herself into a serpent, echoes closely the fight between the Red Crosse Knight and the monstrous half-woman, half-serpent Error (*FQ* I. i. 18–19).[16] As well as a taste of Heaven, and a taste of virtue, this Chronicle also seems intent on giving the reader a taste for literature.

And a taste for philosophy. Although *The Silver Chair* makes it plain that reason alone is not enough, clear thinking is nevertheless required. The crucial dialogue between the Witch and the heroes of *The Silver Chair* is about appearance and reality, with the Witch representing a materialist, reductionist position, according to which anything outside of Underland (including the sun and Aslan himself) is merely an imagined copy or projection of some 'reality' in Underland (in this case, a lamp and a cat). However, the Witch does not rely on the force of logic, but rather on the hypnotic effect of her playing on a kind of mandolin, and the fumes from a magic powder she throws on the fire, both of which make it 'harder to think' (*SC* 238). The Witch is on the brink of victory, with Rilian and the children having lost almost all memory of 'the real world', when Puddleglum saves the day, not by any decisive turn of argument, but by *doing* 'a very brave thing'. He stamps out the fire. This action is effective not only because it stops the befuddling fumes, but also because 'the pain itself made Puddleglum's head for a moment perfectly clear and he knew exactly what he really thought' (*SC* 144). The action also has a symbolic resonance because in Plato's allegory it is the fire in the cave which produces illusion. The clear-headed Puddleglum then addresses the Witch as follows:

> Suppose we *have* only dreamed, or made up, all these things – trees and grass and sun and moon and Aslan himself. Then all I can say is that... the made-up things seem a good deal more important than the real ones.... We're just babies making up a game, if you're right. But four babies... can make a play-world that licks your real world hollow. That's why I'm going to stand by the play-world. I'm on Aslan's side even if there isn't any Aslan to lead it. I'm going to live as like a Narnian as I can even if there isn't any Narnia. (*SC* 145)

Just as Plato provides an explanation of his Cave allegory, Lewis could also be seen as providing an explanation of this scene in *The Silver Chair* in his paper 'On Obstinacy in Belief', given at the Oxford Socratic Club in 1955. Almost as a belated response to Elizabeth Anscombe, Lewis discusses the place of logic and evidence in religious belief. He concludes with a sentence which seems to sum up in cold prose what Puddleglum says with unaccustomed passion:

> They [the critics of religious belief] cannot be expected to see how the *quality* of the object [God] which we think we are beginning to know... drives us to the view that if this were a delusion then we would have to say that the universe had produced no real thing of comparable value and that all explanations of the delusion seemed somehow less important than the thing explained. (*TAP* 196, emphasis in original)

This is a far cry from the confident rational certainty of the chapter on 'The Self-Contradiction of the Naturalist' in the original version of *Miracles*, and perhaps closer than Lewis acknowledges to the philosophy of 'As If' and the philosophical Pragmatism which he refused to take seriously there. An older and possibly wiser Lewis is willing to entertain the truth-value of the aesthetic: 'The assumption . . . that the ethical is the aesthetic *par excellence* is so basic to Sidney that he never argues it. He thought we ought to know' (*EL* 346).

Finally, it is worth noting that Lewis's lost mother also appears in *The Silver Chair*. Rilian's mother is poisoned by the Green Witch in the form of a serpent. When Rilian reaches her, 'at the first glance of her face Rilian knew that no physic in the world would do her any good' (*SC* 50). This sentence points both forward to Digory's dying mother in *The Magician's Nephew*, and back to Jack's dying mother in Belfast. Rilian sets off to avenge his mother's death – that is, to come to terms with it; but in vain. Instead he is ensnared for ten years by the witch-woman described by one critic as 'his ambiguous paramour/step-mother'.[17] It is tempting to speculate about the fact that roughly ten years elapsed between Lewis's moving in with Mrs Moore and his conversion to Christianity, with the probable termination of whatever sexual relations there may have been between them. The crucial events in Rilian's liberation – the extinguishing of the fire, the recovery of a clear head, and the commitment to 'myth' (the 'play-world' that 'licks the real world hollow') – could all be related to Lewis's conversion. These similarities can be put down to chance, though we may suspect, along with Freud and the Hermit in *The Horse and His Boy*, that there is no such thing as an accident (*HHB* 118).

THE HORSE AND HIS BOY

The Horse and His Boy was written before *The Silver Chair*, but published after it in order to maintain the continuity of the three Chronicles involving Caspian. Indeed, *The Horse and His Boy* is referred to in *The Silver Chair* as the 'grand old tale of Prince Cor and Aravis and the horse Bree' which is recited by the blind poet as the entertainment at a banquet in Cair Paravel (*SC* 41). The tale is set in 'the Golden Age when Peter was High King'; in Narnian terms, the tale is a 'classic'. However, in terms of the seven *Chronicles of Narnia*, *The Horse and His Boy* is the lightest, almost a *divertissement* before the much weightier narratives of the Creation and End of Narnia in *The Magician's Nephew* and *The Last Battle* respectively. While Aslan does feature significantly in *The Horse and His Boy*, there is a relative lack of the supernatural in the book. It is much more of a straight adventure story, with a rags-to-riches motif as Shasta, the poor fisherman's boy, turns out to be Prince (later King) Cor of Archenland. The book is perhaps more overtly moralizing than the others, with Lewis's particular target being pride or arrogance, as displayed in varying degrees by Rabadash, the headstrong Calormene prince; by Aravis, the runaway Calormene noblewoman; and by Bree, the Talking Horse returning to his roots in Narnia. Myers makes a good case for *The Horse and His Boy* being Lewis's 'miniature book of courtesy', based on book VI of *The Faerie Queene*.[18] For Lewis, as for Spenser, courtesy is not a matter of outward rules of etiquette (such merely external courtesy is ridiculed in the hypocritical verbosity of the Calormene courtiers), but is 'the poetry of conduct . . . the bloom . . . on the virtues of charity and humility' (*AOL* 351–2). The principal exponents of the latter virtues are the Hermit (as in Spenser) and Hwin, also a Narnian Talking Horse, who 'belongs' to Aravis.

The last phrase touches on one of the key motifs of the book (and apparent in the joke in the book's title): the 'normal' relation between horse and rider is subverted, and it is the horses who are at least as much in charge of their riders as vice versa. While Lewis had undoubtedly read his Swift ('Hwin' is surely a Houhynhym, as Holbrook says), one also wonders whether he had read Tolstoy's 'Kholstomer', a tale told from the point of view of the horse, and referred to in Victor Shklovsky's famous essay on defamiliarization, 'Art as Technique'. Certainly there is an element of defamiliarization when the hierarchical Calormene world is subverted by the Talking Horses, as in the scene when Bree addresses Aravis: '"Hwin isn't *your* horse any longer. One might just as well say you're *her* human." The girl opened her mouth to speak and then stopped. Obviously she had not quite seen it in that light before' (*HHB* 33, emphasis in original).

But there is little doubt who is really in charge in *The Horse and His Boy*. Aslan, incognito as he accompanies Shasta over the dark mountains, reveals that *he* was the lion who forced him to join with Aravis; *he* was the cat who comforted him among the tombs of Tashbaan; *he* was the lion who chased the travellers in order to hurry them up; *he* was the one who guided the infant Cor to the shore where the poor fisherman Arsheesh found him. When Shasta asks who 'he' is, 'the Voice' replies three times: 'Myself' (*HHB* 130). This episode has been interpreted as the closest Lewis gets to an explicit Trinitarian theology in *The Chronicles of Narnia*. There is, despite the lightness of the tale, a heavy theological presence lurking in this book. And Aslan's justice can be literally heavy-handed. When, in the form of a cat, he sits with Shasta all night by the tombs, Shasta innocently confesses that he once threw stones at a cat. At this, the 'cat' Aslan scratches Shasta. This incident prefigures the scene where Aslan ferociously inflicts ten scratches or tears on Aravis's back as retribution for the whipping given to her slave when Aravis escaped: 'The scratches on your back, tear for tear, throb for throb, blood for blood, are equal to the stripes laid on the back of your stepmother's slave because of the drugged sleep you cast upon her' (*HHB* 158). We have already noted the marked streak of cruelty in the 'undressing' of Eustace in *The Voyage of the 'Dawn Treader'*, which also involved the tearing of a child's flesh by Aslan. In this case, too, there is the suggestion of some kind of sado-masochistic interest, an impression which seems to be confirmed by the immediately preceding exchange between Aslan and Hwin:

> Then Hwin, though shaking all over, gave a strange little neigh, and trotted across to the Lion.
>
> 'Please,' she said, 'you're so beautiful. You may eat me if you like. I'd sooner be eaten by you than fed by anyone else'.
>
> 'Dearest daughter,' said Aslan, planting a lion's kiss on her twitching velvet nose, 'I knew you would not be long in coming to me. Joy shall be yours.' (*HHB* 157–8)

Again, the linking of cruelty and fairly obvious sexual excitement with strong parental and religious overtones (Bree has just been invited, like doubting Thomas, to touch Aslan) may not be to every reader's taste.

THE MAGICIAN'S NEPHEW

Mothers are notable by their absence in *The Horse and His Boy* (by contrast, the *fathers* of Shasta/Cor, Aravis, and Rabadash all figure significantly in the narrative). But in *The Magician's Nephew* the presence of Digory's dying mother is pervasive. Between the introduction in chapter one of the tear-stained boy whose mother is dying, and the moment in chapter eleven when Digory finally asks Aslan for something 'to make Mother well', there are regular reminders (at least ten) of his mother's frail condition. Thus, despite momentous events such as the death and birth of worlds (Charn and Narnia respectively), the reader is never allowed to forget what the story is really about. Lewis could hardly make it clearer that the birth of Narnia is intimately connected with his attempt somehow to come to terms with the death of his mother.

Lewis locates the beginning of *The Magician's Nephew* in Edwardian London – typically, by means of literary references. The reader is taken back into the world of Sherlock Holmes and E. Nesbit's Bastable children; and also, of course, into the world of the young Jack Lewis. Digory's father is abroad, but his Uncle Andrew, far from acting as a good father-substitute for Digory, is cruel, vain, and dangerous, being something of a magician. Digory is thrown back on the support of the girl next door, Polly

Plummer. Together they accidentally stumble into Uncle Andrew's secret chamber. Before the children realize what is happening, Uncle Andrew makes Polly disappear, presumably into another world, by means of a magic ring. Digory is thus compelled to follow her to take her the ring which will bring them home. To Digory's disgust, Uncle Andrew is himself unwilling to try out the magic rings he has made. But before Digory leaves to follow Polly, he is given the history of the rings. Uncle Andrew had inherited from a Mrs Lefay, who was literally his fairy godmother (being 'one of the last mortals in this country who had fairy blood in her'), a box which, it transpired, was of Atlantean origin. Atlantis is, of course, significant for Lewis in that the loss of security he suffered at his mother's death is described in *Surprised by Joy* as being like the sinking of the great continent of Atlantis (*SBJ* 23). In a phrase which suggests far more than its literal meaning, Uncle Andrew says: 'The Atlantean box contained something that had been brought from another world when our world was only just beginning' (*MN* 23). On a literal level, the box contains dust from another world (actually from 'the Wood between the Worlds', though Uncle Andrew does not know this), which he has succeeded in making into magic rings. On a symbolic level, 'the Atlantean box' suggests the 'primary maternal matrix' or Kristeva's semiotic *chora*, from which the beginnings of all human being and identity emerge. *The Magician's Nephew* can be read as an account of Lewis's attempt, in the realm of the imaginary, to return to the primary maternal matrix from which he was 'untimely ripp'd', and to find a new beginning in which that primary loss is more successfully dealt with.

When Digory puts on the ring, he does not find himself in another world, but in what he names 'the Wood between the Worlds', an intermediate place of womb-like 'dreamful ease', where he finds Polly and one of Uncle Andrew's guinea pigs. Having first established, at Polly's sensible insistence, that they can get home, they then decide to explore some of the other worlds which can be entered via the many pools in the Wood. Their first stop is the dead world of Charn, where Digory, because he cannot resist ringing an obviously magical bell, awakens the terrifying witch Jadis from an enchanted sleep. In psychoanalytical terms Jadis can be read as the 'split-off' 'Bad

Mother', the epitome of rejecting cruelty. She is, of course, the White Witch of *The Lion, the Witch and the Wardrobe*, who, unfair as it may seem in rational terms, embodies the feelings of rejection the young Lewis would have had at his mother's death (and perhaps earlier, if Holbrook is right). After a bizarre interlude back in London (Lewis in this book manages a fine balance of terror, pathos, and hilarity), Jadis and the children, now accompanied by Uncle Andrew, a cabby, and a horse named Strawberry, find themselves in utter darkness, in a place 'without form and void'. There they witness the creation of the world of Narnia. It begins with a voice singing. The voice seems to come from all directions at once, and even out of the earth: 'Its lower notes were deep enough to be the voice of the earth herself [*sic*]. There were no words. There was hardly even a tune. But it was, beyond comparison, the most beautiful noise he [Digory] had ever heard. It was so beautiful he could hardly bear it' (*MN* 93). As the Voice sings into existence first stars, and then a sun, the children and the cabby can be seen with faces filled with joy, looking as if the sound 'reminded them of something' (*MN* 94–5). While this scene clearly echoes the biblical Creation myth, there are also echoes of another myth of origins, that told by psychoanalysts such as Winnicott and Kristeva, where the individual comes into being in the play of the mother's voice and eyes and body. Lewis seems here to be going back into 'the semiotic', the living pulse of song, to find a new beginning with a good mother. This 'good mother' is Aslan (his maleness notwithstanding). In a later passage which echoes the remarkable description of Lewis's first encounter with the 'Holiness' of George MacDonald's *Phantastes*, experienced as an intangible, elusive presence connected with 'the voice of my mother or my nurse' (*SBJ* 145), Lewis gives the following account of Aslan as the semiotic 'Good Mother' (or 'imaginary father'?):

> Both the children were looking up into the Lion's face . . . and all at once . . . the face seemed to be a sea of tossing gold in which they were floating, and such a sweetness and power rolled about them and over them and entered them that they felt that they had never been happy or wise or good, or even alive and awake, before. And the memory of that moment stayed with them always, so that . . . if ever they were sad or afraid or angry, the thought of all that golden goodness, and the feeling that it was still there, quite close, just

> around some corner or just behind some door, would come back and make them sure, deep down inside, that all was well. (*MN* 165)

If Aslan figures as the 'Good Mother', the 'Bad Mother' is well and truly 'abjected' in the figure of Uncle Andrew. Jadis herself simply disappears from Narnia at the end of the book, to reappear hundreds of years later as the White Witch of *The Lion, the Witch and the Wardrobe*. But Uncle Andrew, who, though an insignificant magician by comparison, has nevertheless been closely identified with Jadis at several points in the book (e.g. *MN* 61, 62), comes to a sticky end in Narnia. Kristeva defines the abject as that which is expelled or rejected as psychologically threatening because it is not clearly one thing or another. The newly created talking animals cannot decide whether Uncle Andrew is some kind of animal (perhaps 'a Neevil', one suggests, corrupting Aslan's talk of 'an evil' having entered Narnia) or a tree. The tree party wins, so Uncle Andrew is planted (the right way up, but only just) and watered with continual drenchings from the elephant's trunk. His howling persuades the animals that he is not after all a tree, so he is dug up, caged, and pelted with thistles, nuts, and worms, all with the best intentions, in an attempt to feed him. He is finally reduced to 'a miserable object in muddy clothes, sitting hunched up'. Lewis's description of Uncle Andrew's fate teeters on the brink of the kind of violent cruelty we see at the end of *That Hideous Strength*, where the animals take their revenge on the vivisectors (Uncle Andrew had, in his small way, been one). Lewis tries to keep the scene light-hearted and comic as the cruel and egotistical parent-figure is ritually abused and humiliated. Indeed, Uncle Andrew could almost be seen as the sacrifice which, according to Kristeva, is necessary for the founding of a social order.[19]

Meanwhile Digory has finally dared to approach Aslan to ask for something to cure his dying mother. Aslan shares Digory's grief, but promises nothing. Instead he offers Digory the opportunity to avert the evil he has brought into Narnia in the form of the Witch. Digory is to bring to Aslan an apple from a tree in the garden at the Western end of the World; the seed from this magic apple will grow into a tree which will ward off the Witch for many centuries. Polly accompanies Digory as they fly on the back of Strawberry, transformed into a winged horse, and renamed Fledge. When Digory reaches the garden and plucks the silver apple, he encounters the Witch, who tempts him to eat it himself, and live forever, rather than bringing it to Aslan. Digory has no great difficulty in resisting this temptation. But the next temptation hits him much harder. The Witch suggests he take the apple to his dying mother:

> 'Soon she will be well again. All will be well again. Your home will be happy again. You will be like other boys.'
>
> 'Oh!' gasped Digory as if he had been hurt, and put his hand to his head. For he now knew that the most terrible choice lay before him. (*MN* 150)

As in *Perelandra,* where Maleldil had forbidden the security of the Fixed Land, obedience for its own sake, against all that seems reasonable and humane, is required of Digory. And, as in *Perelandra,* temptation is resisted, and a kind of Fall averted. But the price for Digory is terrible; it seems that he must accept the inevitability of his mother's death. This is a re-enactment of Lewis's childhood trauma, when he had to come to terms with the fact that his prayers for his mother's recovery remained unanswered. In this reprise of Lewis's own early experience, Digory comes to accept that 'there might be things more terrible than losing someone you love by death' (*MN* 163). But, although Digory wins through to acceptance, he is spared the ultimate trial which the young Lewis had to face. Aslan tells him to pluck an apple which *will* heal his mother. For Digory 'it is as if the whole world had turned inside out and upside down' (*MN* 163). This is the 'joyous turn', the *Eucatastrophe,* which Tolkien demanded of the fairy tale, and which brings consolation to the reader.[20] What kind of consolation this imaginary resolution may have brought to the writer is another question.

THE LAST BATTLE

The Last Battle is a profoundly melancholy book. It opens with a depressing vignette of domestic tyranny in which the ruthless ape Shift routinely exploits the good will and gullibility of Puzzle the donkey. Whatever traces it may contain of Lewis's own reputed domestic bondage to Mrs Moore, this opening chapter also anticipates the apocalyptic conclusion of *The Last Battle* when, in the words of the poet Lewis wished to emulate:

> The ceremony of innocence is drowned;
> The best lack all conviction, while the worst
> Are full of passionate intensity.
>
> (W. B.Yeats, 'The Second Coming')

The passivity, and even collusion, of the Talking Animals in the Narnian holocaust evoke the same ambivalent response in the reader as does Puzzle's stupidity. As Edmund says to Puzzle: 'If you'd spent less time saying you weren't clever and more time trying to be as clever as you could...' (*LB* 81).

By the second chapter we are warned by Roonwit the Centaur that 'there have not been such disastrous conjunctions of the planets for five hundred years . . . some great evil hangs over Narnia' (*LB* 19). The discussion between Roonwit, King Tirian, and Jewel the Unicorn about the rumours of Aslan's presence in Narnia are interrupted by the arrival of a dying Dryad who brings news of the felling of talking trees in Lantern Waste. They then discover that the felled trees are being sold to the Calormenes, apparently on Aslan's orders. The horror that is to come begins to dawn on Tirian and Jewel:

> 'Jewel,' [Tirian] said, 'what lies before us? Horrible thoughts arise in my heart. If we had died before today we should have been happy. '
>
> 'Yes,' said Jewel. 'We have lived too long. The worst thing in the world has come upon us'. (*LB* 24)

Shortly after this 'a really dreadful thing' happens. Tirian and Jewel come across two Calormenes whipping a Talking Horse; enraged, they kill the Calormenes without warning. Tirian feels that he is dishonoured, and must surrender himself to the Calormenes to be brought before Aslan. He realizes that he is going to his death, but asks: 'Would it not be better to be dead than to have this horrible fear that Aslan has come and it is not like the Aslan we believed in and longed for? It is as if the sun rose one day and were a black sun' (*LB* 29). This echoes the image of 'the black sun of melancholy' in Gérard de Nerval's poem 'El Desdichado' (The Disinherited One), which Julia Kristeva takes for the title of her book *Black Sun: Depression and Melancholia*. Whether or not Lewis knew Nerval's poem, he would certainly have encountered the 'black-sun' image in George MacDonald's *Phantastes*.[21] Kristeva's analysis of the melancholy inscribed in Nerval's poem seems to fit Lewis's life and work uncannily well. The prince in Nerval's poem is disinherited not of a 'property' or 'object', but of 'an unnameable domain... the secret and unreachable horizon of our loves and desires... [which] assumes, for the imagination, the consistency of an archaic mother'.[22] The loss which is really being mourned in *The Last Battle* is not so much that of Narnia as that of Atlantis, the 'archaic mother', whose sinking has caused Lewis inconsolable grief. As Kristeva puts it: 'The melancholy does not pass. Neither does the poet's past'.[23]

The Last Battle depicts a losing battle against despair. Hope keeps reviving, but only to be dashed. The real villains are the dwarfs. The first turning point is when Tirian, Jill, Eustace, *et al.* rescue a party of dwarfs being marched off to the Calormene mines. But, instead of rejoicing at their liberation, and at the revelation that the new 'bad' Aslan is in reality just Puzzle dressed up by Shift in a lion skin, the dwarfs are deeply cynical: 'No more Aslan, no more Kings, no more silly stories about other worlds', they say (*LB* 72). Whatever political point may be being made here, for Lewis what is really at issue is the power of the imagination to transfigure a harsh reality. The second turning point comes during the Last Battle itself, when the hard-pressed Narnians are about to be reinforced by a detachment of Talking Horses. The horses are destroyed by the archery of the dwarfs. This really is the end. Inevitably the heroes are forced into the stable at the centre of the battle. The stable is for them the jaws of death, for it contains Tash, the hideous monster worshipped by the Calormenes.

If ever anything was, to use Tolkien's term, a '*dyscatastrophe*', this is it. It seems the end of Narnia, and of all the joy it has brought. But, in a final turn of 'sudden and miraculous grace', *dyscatastrophe* is turned into 'the joy of deliverance', a deliverance which 'denies (in the face of much evidence, if you will) universal final defeat and in so far is *evangelium* [good news], giving a fleeting glimpse of Joy, Joy beyond the walls of the world, poignant as grief'.[24] But this turn to Joy is to be no brief encounter. While the stable does contain Tash, who rapidly disappears with the Calormene chief tucked under two of his four arms, it also contains Heaven itself, Aslan's country. In a reprise of Lucy's first experience in the wardrobe, it turns out that 'its inside is bigger than its outside'. But this time it seems it cannot be Narnia that is through the door, because the door leads *from* Narnia into somewhere else (and, in a magnificent pastiche of the biblical Apocalypse, the children witness the end of Narnia as they look back through the door). Yet the 'somewhere else' is strangely reminiscent of Narnia. As Professor Digory Kirke, who has mysteriously turned up along with the other friends of Narnia, realizes, this world is in Platonic terms 'the real Narnia', of which the vanished Narnia was only the shadow or copy (*LB* 159–60). The company of true Narnians rushes ever 'further up and further in' until they arrive at the 'real' Narnian equivalent of the Western garden which the young Digory had visited with Polly in *The Magician's Nephew.* But once again 'the inside is larger than the outside', for the garden contains yet another 'Narnia' which is even more beautiful and more real than the Narnia they have just left, just as *that* Narnia was more beautiful and real than the Narnia left behind through the stable door (*LB* 169).

This journey from glory to glory, ever further up and further in, embodies the vision of Christian Platonism. Discussion of its theological adequacy is beyond the scope of the present book. The question which concerns us here is whether, in this very grand finale, the broken heart of the little boy from Belfast is finally mended. That little boy haunts the pages of *The Chronicles of Narnia,* until at the end of *The Magician's Nephew* his mother is restored to life by the goodness of Aslan and the power of Narnian magic. But in *The Last Battle* the goodness of Aslan is called in question, and Narnia itself falls. The main doubters of Aslan and his goodness are the dwarfs, who are also pivotal in the fall of Narnia. They too come through the stable door, but refuse to believe in the wonderful new world which the friends of Narnia find. For them, it is simply a pathetic illusion. For them, there is no 'healing of harms'. For them, the children's vision of their dead mother and father waving to them across the valley, as if 'from the deck of a big ship when you are waiting on the quay' (*LB* 170), would be one more piece of wishful thinking. It would be 'all that stuff about family reunions "on the further shore" ... out of bad hymns and lithographs ... it rings false. We *know* it couldn't be like that.' The voice here is not that of the dwarfs, however, but of the narrator in *A Grief Observed,* Lewis's anatomy of his own bereavement at the age of 61 (see *AGO* 23). It seems that the dwarfs (or manikins, as they are sometimes called) are never entirely left behind.

6

Consummatum Est: Tales of Love and Death

The problem posed by the disbelieving dwarfs reappears in Lewis's next piece of fiction, *Till We Have Faces: A Myth Retold*. The myth in question is that of Cupid and Psyche, classically told by Apuleius in his *Metamorphoses* (or *The Golden Ass*). Lewis's retelling of the myth transforms it in several ways. The action described is presented as historical fact, which in the course of the narrative *becomes* myth. The turning point of the narrative comes when Psyche's sister, Orual, the narrator and central character, stumbles across a secluded temple dedicated to Psyche, and hears a priest recite the myth of Cupid and Psyche. This retelling as myth of 'the facts' in which Orual had been a major participant many years before enrages her. A significant difference between the myth and 'what really happened' lies in their diverging accounts of what led Psyche to disobey Cupid's command never to see his face – a disobedience which causes Psyche to lose her divine lover. In the myth, Psyche's disobedience is prompted by her jealous sisters, whereas 'in fact' Orual was never, she insists, motivated by jealousy of Psyche's lover and grand palace. Orual claims only ever to have acted out of love for Psyche. The crucial 'fact' which the myth misses out is that Psyche's palace was *invisible* to Orual, who therefore believed that Psyche needed to be rescued from madness. This omission from 'the sacred story' wipes out 'the very meaning, the pith, the central knot, of the whole tale', says Orual (*TWHF* 252). She therefore resolves to retell the myth 'as it really happened', and this retelling forms the bulk of *Till We Have Faces*. And, since Orual holds the gods responsible for the false myth of Cupid and Psyche, her retelling is also an indictment of the gods. Orual's account is thus the opposite of theodicy; it attacks the divine injustice. It could also be seen as written 'in defence of the dwarfs' – that is, in defence of those who do not, or will not, see the reality of magical palaces, or 'real Narnias', or perfect islands.

As we shall see, it is really Orual who is being put on trial by Lewis and his collaborator on *Till We Have Faces*, Joy Davidman, to whom the book is dedicated. In 1956, the year the book was published, Lewis married Joy in the Oxford Registry Office, ostensibly only in order to secure his American collaborator's continued residence in Britain. But the following year, when Joy appeared to be dying of cancer, Lewis declared his love for her, and they were married in a religious ceremony in an Oxford hospital. As even Lewis himself was to recognize with hindsight, there was something uncannily familiar about the fact that he fell in love with, and married, a dying mother of two boys. However, Joy's remarkable, though temporary, recovery allowed the Lewises to enjoy three years of marital happiness. The precise chronology of the relationship between Lewis and Joy Davidman has been subject to some debate and speculation. However that may be, there is little doubt that, among the several senses in which *Till We Have Faces* can be called a tale of love, it is a tale whose telling grew apace with the growing love between Jack Lewis and Joy Davidman.

The idea of making a version of the Cupid and Psyche myth had been with Lewis for over thirty years, though the most appropriate literary form had eluded him. The close cooperation with Joy seems to have unblocked the stasis into which his creative energies had fallen since the Narnia books. Whatever the contribution made by Joy, who was a published poet and novelist in her own right, *Till We Have Faces* is in form, if not in content, almost unrecognizable as Lewis's work. The Narnia books and *That Hideous Strength* have an omniscient narrator, while *Out of the Silent Planet* and *Perelandra* are narrated by a friend of Ransom who enjoys a remarkable ability to infiltrate another's consciousness; there is no questioning of the narrator's authority in these books. But *Till We Have Faces* has that most characteristic device of the modern novel, an unreliable narrator. Orual's resolve to set the record straight results, of course, only in *her* version of events. Lewis's awareness of the presence of selectivity and bias in any account of 'the facts' may have been heightened by his experience of writing his own story in *Surprised by Joy*, published the year before *Till We Have Faces*. Some commentators have seen the story of Orual, the unsightly workaholic queen tortured by guilt and despair, as a version of Lewis's own story. Others have seen in Orual echoes of Joy Davidman. More likely Orual is a kind of 'Everyman' figure. In the text itself her identity is fluid: she is Psyche; she is Ungit (the Venus of the kingdom of Glome); under her permanent veil she is imagined to be an infinite variety of things, from an animal, to a great beauty, to nothing at all (*TWHF* 237). Like the faceless image of Ungit in the temple, and like the text itself, she is open to interpretation.

More precisely, it is the nature of Orual's *love* which is open to interpretation, and which is the 'central knot in the tale'. In Orual's version, her love for Psyche, and indeed for other characters such as her Greek tutor, Lysias ('the Fox'), and Bardia, her general, is presented as innocent and selfless. By the end of the book, however, her love for each of these characters can be seen as deeply selfish and manipulative. Indeed *Till We Have Faces* could be said to embody in fictional form the gist of Lewis's later book, *The Four Loves*. There Lewis argues that the three natural loves – that is, affection (Greek *storge*), friendship (Greek *philia*), and *eros* – all tend to become perverted unless redeemed by the fourth love, divine charity. Orual's love for 'the Fox' exemplifies friendship, her love for Bardia has an erotic dimension, and her love for Psyche is what Lewis calls affection; but in each case Orual's natural human love is shown to have been perverted by her selfishness.

It is Orual's love for Psyche which is the central issue of the book, however. Psyche's mother died giving birth to Psyche, and her older stepsister Orual acted as a mother-substitute to the preternaturally beautiful Psyche. The particular danger of the quasi-maternal love of Orual for Psyche had already been intimated in the ghastly possessive mother in *The Great Divorce*, and will appear later in the sketch of 'Mrs Fidget' in *The Four Loves*, where Lewis writes: 'the ravenous need to be needed will gratify itself either by keeping its objects needy or by inventing for them imaginary needs. It will do this all the more ruthlessly because it thinks (in one sense truly) that it is a Gift-love and therefore regards itself as "unselfish"' (*FL* 63). Orual's 'ravenous need to be needed' begins to appear amid her entirely justified fears for Psyche when the priest of Ungit demands that Psyche be exposed on the mountain as an offering to 'the Shadowbrute' or god of the mountain. What Orual cannot bear is the faint hope Psyche entertains that the god of the mountain may turn out to be the divine lover for whom she has always longed. Psyche's hope for a love-death that will fulfill her *Sehnsucht* evokes intense hostility in Orual (*TWHF* 82 ff.). Thus, when Orual subsequently discovers Psyche alone on the mountain, she is strongly predisposed to disbelieve Psyche's claim that she has indeed come home to her divine lover. The trouble is that this 'home', a fabulous palace, is invisible to Orual. Rather than believe that the palace is real but invisible to her, Orual decides that Psyche is either 'bad' (playing games), or more likely 'mad'.

The 'central knot' of the tale is given a further twist when Orual fleetingly *does* see a fabulous palace, which promptly vanishes (*TWHF* 141–2). This glimpse is perfectly explicable in rational terms, given the swirling mist and Orual's distraught, half-awake condition. Orual is faced with much more ambiguous evidence than are the dwarfs or Lucy's siblings in the Narnia books, where failure to see Aslan or the 'real Narnia' is presented as wilful lack of faith. The extent to which this shift towards an acknowledgement of ambiguity is due to the influence of Joy Davidman is not certain; but certainly both the form and the content of *Till We Have Faces* foreground ambiguity in a way which is new to Lewis. Living with ambivalence can be seen as a mark of psychological maturity. Maybe Lewis's complicated involvement with Joy confirmed that 'getting it right' first time around is not the *sine qua non* of ultimate happiness. Orual finds that she has to retell her retelling of the myth of Psyche. In terms which echo Lewis's own writing of *Surprised by Joy,* she says: 'What began the change was the very writing itself. Let no one lightly set about such a work. Memory, once waked, will play the tyrant' (*TWHF* 263). Subsequent revelations by acquaintances, and in dreams and visions, make Orual despair of catching the truth in 'trim sentences' which are in reality merely 'the babble we think we mean' (*TWHF* 305). Truth is only available to mortals in the indeterminacy of language, where 'like all these sacred matters, it is and is not' (*TWHF* 279). In the end of this tale of love, the tale of Jack Lewis and Joy Davidman as much as of Orual and Psyche, it is impossible finally to know who is who, and who is responsible for what. But, as words fail, Joy comes:

> The air was growing brighter and brighter about us; as if something had set it on fire. Each breath I drew let into me new terror, joy, overpowering sweetness. I was pierced through and through with the arrows of it. I was being unmade. I was no one. But that's little to say; rather, Psyche herself was, in a manner, no one. I loved her as I would have once thought it impossible to love; would have died any death for her. And yet, it was not, not now, she that really counted. Or if she counted (and oh, gloriously she did) it was for another's sake.... The most dreadful, the most beautiful, the only dread, and beauty there is, was coming. (*TWHF* 318–19)

This experience of an intense human love being taken up, without diminishment, into the love of God is transposed from its mythical presentation in *Till We Have Faces* into plain prose in *The Four Loves* (see *FL* 158). The relevant passage in the latter occurs in the context of a discussion of the destiny of human love 'in Heaven'. Lewis could hardly have been unaware that this discussion of love after death was uncomfortably close to his situation with Joy, whose cancer was at this time in remission. Nevertheless speculation about one's post-mortem relationship with 'the Beloved' in the innocuous counters of a theological discussion is far removed from the reality of having to come to terms with feelings of grief for a dead spouse. Yet a mere five months after the publication of *The Four Loves*, Lewis was again writing about love after death, only this time for real. The origins of *A Grief Observed* lie in the jottings Lewis made about his own reactions to Joy's death in the summer of 1960. However, *A Grief Observed* is not directly autobiographical. It is a fictionalized version of Lewis's experience. There can be no doubt that Lewis *is* talking about his own experience, yet there are devices which distance the narrative voice from a direct identification with Lewis's: Joy becomes 'H' (Helen was Joy's middle name); the narrator refers to some 'very ancient arithmetic by J[ack]'at the end of the notebook he is using (*AGO* 47); and the book was originally published under the pseudonym N. W. Clerk (though it appeared under Lewis's own name after his death).

A Grief Observed is a tale of love and death – a 'tale' not only in the sense that it is presented as fiction (however transparently grounded in fact), but also in the sense that it tells the *story* of a grief. Sorrow, we are told, 'turns out to be not a state but a *process*. It needs not a map but a history' (*AGO* 47, emphasis added). Although initially this record of grief was 'a defence against total collapse, a safety-valve' (*AGO* 47), and consists of a series of loosely connected fragments, nervertheless its terse style and abrupt shifts of direction have a narrative quality reminiscent of *Till We Have Faces*. While the book does mention 'the laziness of grief' (*AGO* 8), and feelings of 'being mildly concussed', with a 'sort of invisible blanket between the world and me' (*AGO* 7), overall it evinces a sense of restless energy. From the opening line: 'No one ever told me that grief felt so like fear', the short and devastatingly lucid sentences hook the reader into a narrative which is driven by a rage to understand, or somehow to come to terms with, the reality of death.

Like *Till We Have Faces* and Lewis's later works generally, *A Grief Observed* foregrounds the radical subjectivity and fallibility of human understanding, 'the idea that I, or any mortal at any time, may be utterly mistaken as to the situation he is really in' (*AGO* 51). The text continues in a sceptical mode: 'Five senses; an incurably abstract intellect; a haphazardly selective memory; a set of preconceptions and assumptions so numerous that I can never examine more than a minority of them – never become even conscious of them all. How much of total reality can such an apparatus let through?' (*AGO* 51). Yet such epistemological uncertainty does not destroy the ontological conviction that there is in the end a 'total reality' to be experienced. Lewis's commitment to the *fact* of reality, unimaginable though that reality may be, separates him from currently fashionable varieties of anti-realism, as well as from the cruder scepticisms of his own day. The way we encounter reality is in its smashing of the images we fabricate of it: 'All reality is iconoclastic' (*AGO* 52).

This self-assertion of the real has its most powerful impact in the realm of personal relationships. As 'Lewis' puts it: 'The most precious gift that marriage gave me was this constant impact of something very close and intimate yet all the time unmistakably other, resistant – in a word, real' (*AGO* 18). And later: 'The earthly beloved... incessantly triumphs over your mere idea of her' (*AGO* 52). But now 'the rough, sharp, cleansing tang of her otherness is gone' (*AGO* 19), and it is 'her foursquare and independent reality' that we are to love after she is dead, not some image or memory (*AGO* 52).

Yet, despite the almost violent rhetoric of 'roughness' and 'resistance' and 'shattering' and 'triumph', what Lewis is recommending can also be expressed in an altogether different register, as the quiet *attention* to what is. The difference between novels and real life, we are told, is that in real life the words and acts of a man are, 'if we observe closely, hardly ever "in character", that is, in what we call his character' (*AGO* 53). Here Lewis seems close to his fellow Platonists Simone Weil and Iris Murdoch in his insistence on the need to attend to the real, which is constantly obscured by the self-protective fantasies ('pasteboard palaces') we create. And Lewis shares the Platonist ambivalence about images in general and art in particular. Life and death may be more real than novels, but this truth is conveyed to us in the artifice of a fictional text. It is typical of Lewis – that most intertextual of beings – to write a story about the uselessness of stories in face of the reality of death, and to offer at the final moment of truth – a literary quotation! The words in Italian which conclude *A Grief Observed* are from Dante's *Paradiso* (Canto XXXI, l. 93). They describe the moment when Beatrice smiles and turns to God, 'the eternal fountain'. The death of 'H' is thus conflated with the beatification of Beatrice. It also recalls the culminating vision of Orual (quoted above), and Orual's final words in a book which is, like *A Grief Observed*, a book in search of an answer: 'I ended my first book with the words *No answer*. I know now, Lord, why you utter no answer. You are yourself the answer. Before your face questions die away' (*TWHF* 319).

Lewis's final book is also situated on the borderline between 'fact' and 'fiction'. In the early 1950s he had attempted, and then abandoned, a book on prayer. Ten years later, he transposed his thoughts on prayer into an imaginary correspondence between 'Lewis' and a character called Malcolm. In *Letters to Malcolm: Chiefly on Prayer*, published in the year after Lewis's death, 'Lewis' says (rather archly):

> But however badly needed a good book on prayer is, I shall never try to write it. Two people on the foothills comparing notes in private

are all very well. But in a book one would inevitably seem to be attempting, not discussion, but instruction. And for me to offer the world instruction about prayer would be an impudence. (*LTM* 66)

In contrast with the stress on 'objectivity' in his early book *The Personal Heresy*, Lewis's late works, such as *An Experiment in Criticism* and *Letters to Malcolm*, show much more interest in questions of subjectivity. Letter XV of *Letters to Malcolm* gives an extended discussion of the 'constructedness' of both self and world; both are 'façades', 'mere surfaces'. In a way which seems to approach some versions of pragmatism or postmodernism, 'Lewis' suggests that all we can wisely do is accept the façades and surfaces *as* façades and surfaces (*LTM* 81). However, 'Lewis' is a realist in that he believes in a 'real but unknown I' behind the façade of the self, and in a 'totally unimaginable' but 'sheerly real' mystery behind the 'stage set' of the world (*LTM* 80 ff.). Both roots of 'the daily miracle of finite consciousness' – that is, the mystery of the real self and that of the real world – 'leap forth from God's naked hand' (*LTM* 81) at some transcendent point inaccessible to anyone 'in the flesh' (*LTM* 83). But for 'Lewis' 'the moment of prayer' does allow, if not an escape from finitude, at least an intense awareness of finitude *as* finitude. If prayer can 're-awake the awareness of that [finite] situation... there is no need to go anywhere else. The situation itself, is, at every moment, a possible theophany. Here is the holy ground, the Bush is burning now' (*LTM* 83). Lewis's first 'theophany' or access of Joy came, of course, at the sight of a flowering currant bush (*SBJ* 18–19). While Lewis never loses sight of the transcendent otherness of a God who constantly shatters the images or ideas we have of him (e.g. *LTM* 84), his last book is pervaded by a gentler sense of the immanence of God. This sense of God cannot be caught in prose but only in poetic images; indeed, not so much in nouns as in adjectives. As 'Lewis' says: 'All my deepest, and certainly all my earliest, experiences seem to be of sheer quality. The terrible and the lovely are older and solider than terrible and lovely things. If a musical phrase could be translated into words at all it would become an adjective' (*LTM* 84). This 'thirst for quality' can be satisfied in prayer, which sometimes brings 'a wave of images, thrown off like spray from the prayer, all momentary, all correcting, refining, "interanimating" one another, and giving a kind of spiritual body to the unimaginable…' (*LTM* 88).

In Letter XVII on 'prayer as worship or adoration' 'Lewis' discusses 'the secret doctrine that *pleasures* are shafts of the glory as it strikes our sensibility' (*LTM* 91; emphasis in original). No pleasure should be too ordinary or too usual to become 'a tiny theophany', which sets the mind running 'back up the sunbeam to the sun' (*LTM* 91–2). Yet 'Lewis' recognizes the danger of being fey, and of overstating what one might call this 'mysticism of the everyday'. He writes:

> Doesn't the mere fact of putting something into words of itself involve an exaggeration? Prose words, I mean. Only poetry can speak low enough to catch the faint murmur of the mind… The other day I tried to describe to you a very minimal experience – the tiny wisps of adoration with which (sometimes) I salute my pleasures. But I now see that putting it down in black and white made it sound far bigger than it really is. The truth is, I haven't any language weak enough to depict the weakness of my spiritual life. If I weakened it enough it would cease to be language at all. (*LTM* 113)

Such an unemphatic spirituality could hardly be further removed from the rhetoric and belligerence of the 1940s Lewis, the Defender of the Faith. The older 'Lewis' of *Letters to Malcolm* writes of his propensity to theological argument: 'It is like taking a red coal out of the fire to examine it: it becomes a dead coal. To me, I mean. All this is autobiography, not theology' (*LTM* 107). In the end, the core of Lewis's *œuvre* is Jack Lewis's quest for Joy, and his love of the dance and play, the truant frivolity, which are the only adequate expression on earth of the Joy that is 'the serious business of Heaven' (*LTM* 95).

Notes

CHAPTER 1. THE QUEST FOR JOY (OR THE DIALECTIC OF DESIRE)

1. Owen Barfield, Introduction, in Jocelyn Gibb (ed.), *Light on C. S. Lewis* (London: Geoffrey Bles, 1965), p. xi.
2. Catherine Belsey, *Desire: Love Stories in Western Culture* (Oxford: Blackwell, 1994), 5.
3. Julia Kristeva, *Tales of Love* (New York: Colombia University Press, 1987), 7.
4. Belsey, *Desire*, 5.
5. Kathryn Lindskoog, *The C. S. Lewis Hoax* (Portland, Or.: Multnomah Press, 1988), 64 ff.
6. George Sayer, *A Life of C. S. Lewis* (London: Hodder & Stoughton, 1997), 154.
7. Ibid., p. xvii.
8. A. N. Wilson, *C. S. Lewis: A Biography* (London: Collins, 1990), p. xvi.
9. Ibid. 58.
10. Lindskoog, *The C. S. Lewis Hoax*, 64.
11. J. R. R. Tolkien, 'On Fairy-Stories', in *Tree and Leaf* (London: Allen & Unwin, 1964), 49.

CHAPTER 2. INTERTEXTUAL HEALING

1. See Walter Hooper, *C. S. Lewis: A Companion and Guide* (London: HarperCollins, 1996), 412–13.
2. Nevill Coghill, 'The Approach to English', in Jocelyn Gibb (ed.), *Light on C. S. Lewis* (London: Geoffrey Bles, 1965), 61.
3. A. N. Wilson, *C. S. Lewis: A Biography* (London: Collins, 1990), 145.
4. Doris T. Myers, *C. S. Lewis in Context* (Kent, Oh.: Kent State University Press, 1994), 126.

5. Wilson, *C. S. Lewis*, 291.
6. See William Gray, 'George MacDonald, Julia Kristeva and the Black Sun', in *Studies in English Literature 1500–1900* (Autumn, 1996), 878 and *passim*.

CHAPTER 3. TELLING IT SLANT: THE ALLEGORICAL IMPERATIVE

1. Catherine Belsey, *Desire: Love Stories in Western Culture* (Oxford: Blackwell, 1994), 152.
2. See Paul Piehler, 'Visions and Revisions: C. S. Lewis's Contributions to the Theory of Allegory', in Bruce L. Edwards (ed.), *The Taste of the Pineapple: Essays on C. S. Lewis as Reader, Critic and Imaginative Writer* (Bowling Green, Oh.: Bowling Green State University Popular Press, 1988), 79.
3. See Paul Piehler, 'Myth or Allegory? Archetype and Transcendence in the Fiction of C. S. Lewis', in Peter J. Schakel and Charles A. Huttar (eds.), *Word and Story in C. S. Lewis* (Columbia, Mo.: University of Missouri Press, 1991).
4. J. R. R. Tolkien, 'On Fairy-Stories', in *Tree and Leaf* (London: Allen & Unwin, 1964), 49.
5. Ibid. 61–2.
6. George Sayer, *A Life of C. S. Lewis* (London: Hodder & Stoughton, 1997), 254.
7. Humphrey Carpenter, *The Inklings: C. S. Lewis, J. R. R. Tolkien, Charles Williams and their Friends* (London: Allen & Unwin, 1978; London: HarperCollins, 1997), 182.
8. Roger Lancelyn Green and Walter Hooper, *C. S. Lewis: A Biography* (London: Collins, 1974), 163.
9. Ibid. 170.

CHAPTER 4. TELLING IT (ALMOST) STRAIGHT: APOLOGIES

1. Austin Farrer, 'The Christian Apologist', in Jocelyn Gibb (ed.), *Light on C. S. Lewis* (London: Geoffrey Bles, 1965), 34.
2. Ibid. 36.
3. Ibid. 40.
4. Ibid. 42.
5. Farrer, in ibid. 25.
6. Jacques Derrida, 'Structure, Sign and Play in the Discourse of the

Human Sciences' (1967), in David Lodge (ed.), *Modern Criticism and Theory: A Reader* (London: Longman, 1988), 279.

7. Humphrey Carpenter, *The Inklings: C. S. Lewis, J. R. R. Tolkien, Charles Williams and their Friends* (London: Allen & Unwin, 1978; London: HarperCollins, 1997), 217.
8. Quoted by Richard L. Purtill, 'Did C. S. Lewis Lose his Faith?', in Andrew Walker and James Patrick (eds.), *A Christian for All Christians: Essays in Honour of C. S. Lewis* (London: Hodder & Stoughton, 1990), 51.
9. George Sayer, *A Life of C. S. Lewis* (London: Hodder & Stoughton, 1997), 308.
10. Quoted by Edward G. Zogby, 'Triadic Patterns in Lewis's Life and Thought', in Peter J. Schakel (ed.), *The Longing for a Form: Essays in the Fiction of C. S. Lewis* (Kent, Oh.: Kent State University Press, 1977), 21.
11. A. N. Wilson, *C. S. Lewis: A Biography* (London: Collins, 1990), 202.

CHAPTER 5. THE CHRISTIAN IMAGINARY: NARNIA

1. J. R. R. Tolkien, 'On Fairy-Stories', in *Tree and Leaf* (London: Allen & Unwin, 1964), 50 ff.
2. See A. N. Wilson, *C. S. Lewis: A Biography* (London: Collins, 1990), 216.
3. See Doris T. Myers, *C. S. Lewis in Context* (Kent, Oh.: Kent State University Press, 1994), 227.
4. Tolkien, 'On Fairy-Stories', 61.
5. Ibid. 66.
6. Ibid. 61.
7. Ibid. 62.
8. See ibid.
9. Ibid.
10. See William Gray, 'George MacDonald, Julia Kristeva and the Black Sun', in *Studies in English Literature 1500–1900* (Autumn, 1996), 892, n. 6.
11. See William Gray, 'The Angel in the House of Death: Gender and Subjectivity in George MacDonald's *Lilith*', in Anne Hogan and Andrew Bradstock (eds.), *Women of Faith in Victorian Culture: Reassessing 'the Angel in the House'* (London: Macmillan, 1998).
12. See Gray, 'George MacDonald, Julia Kristeva and the Black Sun'.
13. Myers, *C. S. Lewis in Context*, 140 ff.
14. Walter Hooper, *C. S. Lewis: A Companion and Guide* (London: HarperCollins, 1996), 438.
15. John D. Cox, 'Epistemological Release in *The Silver Chair*', in Peter

J. Schakel (ed.), *The Longing for a Form: Essays in the Fiction of C. S. Lewis* (Kent, Oh.: Kent State University Press, 1977).

16. See ibid. 161–2.
17. Ibid. 163.
18. Myers, *C. S. Lewis in Context*, 157.
19. John Lechte, *Julia Kristeva* (London: Routledge, 1990), 73 ff., 148–9.
20. Tolkien, 'On Fairy-Stories', 60.
21. See Gray, 'George MacDonald, Julia Kristeva and the Black Sun', 885 and *passim*.
22. Julia Kristeva, *Black Sun: Depression and Melancholia* (New York: Columbia University Press, 1989), 145.
23. Ibid. 165.
24. Tolkien, 'On Fairy-Stories', 60.

Select Bibliography

SELECT LIST OF WORKS BY C. S. LEWIS

There is a full bibliography of works by C. S. Lewis in Walter Hooper, *C. S. Lewis: A Companion and Guide* (London: HarperCollins, 1996). In the following select bibliography I have listed the first edition, followed by the edition I have used.

Spirits in Bondage: A Cycle of Lyrics (under the pseudonym of Clive Hamilton) (London: Heinemann, 1919).

Dymer (under the pseudonym of Clive Hamilton) (London: Dent, 1926; repr. with a Preface in 1950).

The Pilgrim's Regress: An Allegorical Apology for Christianity, Reason and Romanticism (London: Dent, 1933; London: Collins Fount, 1977).

The Allegory of Love: A Study in Medieval Tradition (Oxford: Clarendon Press, 1936; repr. with corrections, London: Oxford University Press, 1938).

Out of the Silent Planet (London: John Lane The Bodley Head, 1938); in *The Cosmic Trilogy* (London: Pan Books in association with The Bodley Head, 1989).

Rehabilitations and Other Essays (London: Oxford University Press, 1939); several of these essays repr. in *Selected Literary Essays*, ed. W. Hooper (Cambridge University Press, 1969).

The Personal Heresy: A Controversy with E. M. W. Tillyard (London: Oxford University Press, 1939).

The Problem of Pain (London: The Centenary Press, 1940; London: Collins Fontana, 1957).

The Screwtape Letters (London: Geoffrey Bles, 1942; London: Collins Fontana, 1955).

A Preface to 'Paradise Lost' (London: Oxford University Press, 1942; London: Oxford Paperbacks, 1960).

Perelandra (London: John Lane The Bodley Head, 1943); in *The Cosmic Trilogy* (London: Pan Books in association with The Bodley Head, 1989).

The Abolition of Man (London: Oxford University Press, 1943; London: Collins Fount, 1978).

That Hideous Strength: A Modern Fairy-Tale for Grown-Ups (London: John Lane The Bodley Head, 1945); in *The Cosmic Trilogy* (London: Pan Books in association with The Bodley Head, 1989).

The Great Divorce: A Dream (London: Geoffrey Bles, 1946; London: Collins Fontana, 1972).

George MacDonald: An Anthology (London: Geoffrey Bles, 1946).

Miracles: A Preliminary Study (London: Geoffrey Bles, 1947; published with a revised chapter III by Collins Fontana in 1960).

The Lion, the Witch and the Wardrobe (London: Geoffrey Bles, 1950; London: HarperCollins Diamond, 1997).

Prince Caspian: The Return to Narnia (London: Geoffrey Bles, 1951; London: HarperCollins Diamond, 1997).

Mere Christianity: A Revised and Amplified Edition, with a New Introduction, of the Three Books 'Broadcast Talks', 'Christian Behaviour' and 'Beyond Personality' (London: Geoffrey Bles, 1952; London: Collins Fontana, 1955).

The Voyage of the 'Dawn Treader' (London: Geoffrey Bles, 1952; London: HarperCollins Diamond, 1997).

The Silver Chair (London: Geoffrey Bles, 1953; London: HarperCollins Diamond, 1997).

The Horse and His Boy (London: Geoffrey Bles, 1954; London: HarperCollins Diamond, 1997).

English Literature in the Sixteenth Century Excluding Drama (The Oxford History of English Literature 3; Oxford: Clarendon Press, 1954; London: Oxford Paperbacks, 1973).

The Magician's Nephew (London: The Bodley Head, 1955; London: HarperCollins Diamond, 1997).

Surprised by Joy: The Shape of my Early Life (London: Geoffrey Bles, 1955; London: Collins Fontana, 1959).

The Last Battle (London: The Bodley Head, 1956; London: HarperCollins Diamond, 1997).

Till We Have Faces: A Myth Retold (London: Geoffrey Bles, 1956; London: Collins Fount, 1978).

Reflections on the Psalms (London: Geoffrey Bles, 1958).

The Four Loves (London: Geoffrey Bles, 1960).

Studies in Words (Cambridge: Cambridge University Press, 1960).

A Grief Observed (under the pseudonym of N. W. Clerk) (London: Faber & Faber, 1961; repr. under Lewis's name in 1964; London: Faber Paperbacks, 1966).

An Experiment in Criticism (Cambridge: Cambridge University Press, 1961; CUP paperback, 1965).

They Asked for a Paper: Papers and Addresses (London: Geoffrey Bles, 1962).

Letters to Malcolm: Chiefly on Prayer (London: Geoffrey Bles, 1964; London: Collins Fount, 1977).

The Discarded Image: An Introduction to Medieval and Renaissance Literature (Cambridge: Cambridge University Press, 1964).

Screwtape Proposes a Toast and Other Pieces (London: Collins Fontana, 1965).

Studies in Medieval and Renaissance Literature, ed. W. Hooper (Cambridge: Cambridge University Press, 1966).

Letters of C. S. Lewis, ed. with a Memoir, by W. H. Lewis (London: Geoffrey Bles, 1966; rev. and enlarged edition, ed. W. Hooper, London: Collins Fount, 1988).

Christian Reflections, ed. W. Hooper (London: Geoffrey Bles, 1967; also London: Collins Fount, 1981; Grand Rapids, Mich.: Eerdmans, 1967).

Spenser's Images of Life, ed. A. Fowler (Cambridge: Cambridge University Press, 1967).

Narrative Poems, ed. W. Hooper (London: Geoffrey Bles, 1969; also London: HarperCollins Fount, 1994).

Selected Literary Essays, ed. W. Hooper (Cambridge: Cambridge University Press, 1969).

Undeceptions: Essays on Theology and Ethics (=US *God in the Dock*), ed. W. Hooper (London: Geoffrey Bles, 1971).

Fern-Seed and Elephants and Other Essays on Christianity, ed. W. Hooper (London: Collins Fontana, 1975).

The Dark Tower and Other Stories, ed. W. Hooper (London: Collins, 1975; also London: Collins Fount, 1983).

They Stand Together: The Letters of C. S. Lewis to Arthur Greeves (1914–63), ed. W. Hooper (London: Collins, 1979).

Of This and Other Worlds (=US *On Stories and Other Essays on Literature*, ed. W. Hooper (London: Collins, 1982; also London: Collins Fount, 1984).

Boxen: The Imaginary World of the Young C. S. Lewis, ed. W. Hooper (London: Collins, 1985).

All My Road Before Me: The Diary of C. S. Lewis, ed. W. Hooper (London: HarperCollins, 1991; also London: Collins Fount, 1993).

The Collected Poems of C. S. Lewis, ed. W. Hooper (London: HarperCollins Fount, 1994).

SELECT LIST OF WORKS ABOUT C. S. LEWIS

For books and articles about Lewis and his works, see Joe R. Christopher and Joan K. Ostling, *C. S. Lewis: An Annotated Checklist of Writings about him and his Works* (Kent, Oh.: Kent State University Press, 1974); and, more recently, Susan Lowenberg, *C. S. Lewis: A Reference*

Guide 1972–1988 (New York: G. K. Hall, 1993). In the following select list I have included books which I have found useful (and which I have been able to get hold of!).

Carnell, Corbin Scott, *Bright Shadow of Reality: C. S. Lewis and the Feeling Intellect* (Grand Rapids, Mich.: Eerdmans, 1974). A thorough exploration of the *Sehnsucht* motif in Lewis's writing. The attempt to relate this to contemporary (in 1974) critical and theological concerns is now rather dated.

Carpenter, Humphrey, *The Inklings: C. S. Lewis, J. R. R. Tolkien, Charles Williams and their Friends* (London: Allen & Unwin, 1978; London: HarperCollins, 1997). Informative and readable account of the circle of friends surrounding Lewis. Carpenter doubts whether Lewis's relationship to Mrs Moore was sexual (though in a 1997 radio programme 'Shadowlands: Truth and Fiction', written and presented by Carpenter, he admits he is now convinced by Wilson's argument that it was).

Christopher, Joe R., *C. S. Lewis* (Boston: Twayne Publishers, 1987). A brisk and (for its size) comprehensive survey of the Lewis *œuvre*. It makes (perhaps too) extensive reference to Tolkien and Dante, of whose works a quite detailed knowledge is presupposed.

Downing, David C., *Planets in Peril: A Critical Study of C. S. Lewis's Ransom Trilogy* (Amherst: University of Massachusetts Press, 1992). A thorough and informative study of Lewis's science-fiction trilogy. It links the trilogy with Lewis's other writings, especially his academic work on medieval literature, in an illuminating way.

Edwards, Bruce L. (ed.), *The Taste of the Pineapple: Essays on C. S. Lewis as Reader, Critic, and Imaginative Writer* (Bowling Green, Oh.: Bowling Green State University Popular Press, 1988). A useful collection, especially on Lewis as critic. The essays by Daniel, Hannay, and Piehler are particularly helpful.

Gibb, Jocelyn (ed.), *Light on C. S. Lewis* (London: Geoffrey Bles, 1965). A collection of reminiscences and reflections published not long after Lewis's death. The introduction by Owen Barfield and the essay by Austin Farrer are seminal.

Glover, Donald E., *C. S. Lewis: The Art of Enchantment* (Athens, Oh.: Ohio University Press, 1981). A systematic study of Lewis's fiction based on Lewis's 'theory' of literature as gleaned from his letters, essays, and especially *An Experiment in Criticism*. Glover's approach is rather conservative, being much concerned with 'the organic sanctity of meaning' (*sic*). In contrast to much Lewis criticism, he thinks highly of *That Hideous Strength*.

Green, Roger Lancelyn, and Hooper, Walter, *C. S. Lewis: A Biography* (London: Collins, 1974). The authorized biography. Green was a pupil and friend of Lewis, and closely involved in the writing of the Narnia books. A good source for material relating to the genesis of many of Lewis's works, but too close to Lewis for much critical distance.

Hannay, Patterson Margaret, *C. S. Lewis* (New York: Frederick Ungar, 1981). A useful introduction to Lewis, with a succinct biography, extensive summaries of all his books, and some perceptive critical discussion.

Holbrook, David, *The Skeleton in the Wardrobe: C. S. Lewis's Fantasies: A Phenomenological Study* (London: Associated University Presses, 1991). An exhaustive reading of Lewis's work in terms of Freudian theory (especially the British 'object-relations' school of Klein and Winnicott). Holbrook is right to argue that such an approach fits Lewis's writings remarkably well. However, his approach is too exclusively psychoanalytic, and some particular interpretations are unconvincing.

Hooper, Walter, *Past Watchful Dragons: A Guide to C. S. Lewis's Chronicles of Narnia* (London: Collins Fount, 1980). Very informative about the background to the Narnia books. Contains relevant extracts from Lewis's juvenilia and from his notebooks, including the entire 'Lefay fragment', an early version of *The Magician's Nephew.*

——— *C. S. Lewis: A Companion and Guide* (London: HarperCollins, 1996). Enormously thorough coverage of Lewis's life and works. Somewhat repetitive, and rather dated critically.

Lindskoog, Kathryn, *The C. S. Lewis Hoax* (Portland, Or.: Multnomah Press, 1988). The main target of Lindskoog's acerbic wit is Walter Hooper and his appropriation of Lewis's life and works, under false pretences, according to Lindskoog. A thought-provoking counter-blast to the Hooper version of Lewis, even if there is only a grain of truth in what Lindskoog claims.

Manlove, Colin, *C. S. Lewis: His Literary Achievement* (Basingstoke: Macmillan, 1987). The most sustained and professional assessment of Lewis's literary *œuvre* to date. Good overview of thematic development, with some penetrating 'close reading'.

——— *The Chronicles of Narnia: The Patterning of a Fantastic World* (New York: Twayne Publishers, 1993). A more 'user-friendly' volume than the above, focusing exclusively on the Narnia books. Accomplished and accessible readings of individual Chronicles. Helpfully frank about other studies of Lewis.

Murphy, Brian, *C. S. Lewis* (Starmont Reader's Guide 14, Mercer Island, Wash.: Starmont House, 1983). Focuses on Lewis as a science-fiction writer, with references to Lewis's other works squeezed in. Perceptive 'close reading' of passages from the science-fiction trilogy.

Myers, Doris T., *C. S. Lewis in Context* (Kent, Oh.: Kent State University Press, 1994). Lewis is presented as a defender of 'Christian Humanism' (his attacks on Renaissance Humanism notwithstanding) against the 'empiricism, nominalism and scepticism', of the dominant theories of language and literature in the first half of the twentieth century. Interesting interpretation of the Narnia books as Lewis's 'miniature *Faerie Queene*'.

Rossi, Lee D., *The Politics of Fantasy: C. S. Lewis and J. R. R. Tolkien* (Ann Arbor, Mich.: UMI Research Press, 1984). Does not quite deliver what the title promises, but good on Lewis's 'divided self', and the tension between 'his need to escape from a threatening world into a private world of fantasy and the anxiety he felt over such a solipsistic retreat'.

Sayer, George, *Jack: A Life of C. S. Lewis* (London: Hodder & Stoughton, 1997; previously published as *Jack: C. S. Lewis and his Times*, Macmillan, 1988). An intimate and at times moving account, written by a former pupil and friend of Lewis. In a new introduction for the 1998 edition, Sayer says that he is 'now certain' that Lewis and Mrs Moore were lovers. Sayer is critical of some of A. N. Wilson's claims.

Schakel, Peter J. (ed.), *The Longing for a Form: Essays in the Fiction of C. S. Lewis* (Kent, Oh.: Kent State University Press, 1977). The first significant collection of critical essays on Lewis's fiction. Occasionally a little dated, but generally helpful. The essays by Cox and Tixier are especially good.

——— *Reason and Imagination in C. S. Lewis: A Study of 'Till We Have Faces'* (Grand Rapids, Mich.: Eerdmans, 1984). An exhaustive interpretation of *Till We Have Faces*, framed by a thoughtful and informed reading of Lewis's *œuvre* as a dialectic of reason and imagination.

——— and Huttar, Charles A. (eds.), *Word and Story in C. S. Lewis* (Columbia, Mo.: University of Missouri Press, 1991). This collection of essays focuses on language and narrative, and is at times theoretically sophisticated and quite demanding. The essays by Medcalf and Piehler are particularly impressive.

Urang, Gunnar, *Shadows of Heaven: Religion and Fantasy in the Writing of C. S. Lewis, Charles Williams and J. R. R. Tolkien* (London: SCM Press, 1971). Although this book was published as long ago as 1971, the chapter on Lewis is still well worth reading. Its criticism of Lewis's fantasy writings is thoughtful and at times penetrating.

Walker, Andrew, and Patrick, James (eds.), *A Christian for All Christians: Essays in Honour of C. S. Lewis* (London: Hodder & Stoughton, 1990). This collection has a theological and philosophical emphasis, though some of the essays (e.g. those by Fiddes, Sellin, and Schakel) deal with Lewis's fiction. Basil Mitchell is illuminating on the original context of Lewis's thought, and its contemporary relevance. Purtill's

'Did C. S. Lewis Lose His Faith?' offers a thorough discussion of the Anscombe affair.

Watson, George (ed.), *Critical Thought Series: 1 Critical Essays on C. S. Lewis* (Aldershot: Scolar Press, 1992). A fascinating collection of articles and reviews dating back to 1936, reproduced in facsimile. The collection focuses on Lewis as a literary historian and critic. The excellent introduction by Watson, and A. D. Nuttall's essay 'Jack the Giant-Killer', relate Lewis to subsequent literary theory, of which, says Nuttall, Lewis 'was prescient'.

Wilson, A. N., *C. S. Lewis: A Biography* (London: Collins, 1990; HarperCollins Flamingo, 1991). Widely acclaimed, well written and provocative, Wilson's book links Lewis's life and writings in an illuminating way. George Sayer has challenged some of Wilson's more controversial claims, and accused him of distorting the evidence.

PERIODICALS

There are several periodicals dedicated to C. S. Lewis and his circle:

CSL: The Bulletin of the New York C. S. Lewis Society (1969–).
Mythlore (1969–).
The Chronicle of the Portland C. S. Lewis Society (1972–).
The Lamp-Post of the Southern California C. S. Lewis Society (1974–).
Seven: An Anglo-American Literary Review (1980–).
Inklings-Jahrbuch (1984–).

OTHER WORKS REFERRED TO IN THIS STUDY

Belsey, Catherine, *Desire: Love Stories in Western Culture* (Oxford: Blackwell, 1994).

Cixous, Hélène, 'Sorties' (1975), in David Lodge (ed.), *Modern Criticism and Theory: A Reader* (London: Longman, 1988).

Derrida, Jacques, 'Structure, Sign and Play in the Discourse of the Human Sciences' (1967), in David Lodge, (ed.), *Modern Criticism and Theory: A Reader* (London: Longman, 1988).

Gray, William, 'George MacDonald, Julia Kristeva and the Black Sun', in *Studies in English Literature 1500–1900* (Autumn 1996).

——— 'The Angel in the House of Death: Gender and Subjectivity in George MacDonald's *Lilith*', in Anne Hogan and Andrew Bradstock (eds.), *Women of Faith in Victorian Culture: Reassessing 'the Angel in the House'* (London: Macmillan, 1998).

Kristeva, Julia, *Tales of Love* (New York: Columbia University Press, 1987).

—— *Black Sun: Depression and Melancholia* (New York: Columbia University Press, 1989).

Lechte, John, *Julia Kristeva* (London: Routledge, 1990).

Lodge, David, (ed.), *Modern Criticism and Theory: A Reader* (London: Longman, 1988).

Shklovsky, Victor, 'Art as Technique' (1917), in David Lodge (ed.), *Modern Criticism and Theory: A Reader* (London: Longman, 1988).

Tolkien, J. R. R., 'On Fairy-Stories', in *Tree and Leaf* (London: Allen & Unwin, 1964).

Winnicott, D. W., *Playing and Reality* (London: Tavistock, 1971; Penguin, 1974).

Index